The Ancient
Messianic
Festivals

And The Prophecies They Reveal

By Ken Johnson, Th.D.

Ancient Messianic Festivals
by Ken Johnson, Th.D.

Printed in the United States of America

ISBN 1468193856
EAN-13 978-1468193855

Dedicated in memory of my mother,
Dorothy M. Johnson
1927-2012

Contents

Introduction.. 7
  The Jewish Calendars 10
  The Former and Latter Rain 15
  Weekly Sabbath, Shabbat............................ 20

Former Rain (spring) Festivals 31
  Search for the Leaven, Bedhot Chamets 32
  Passover, Pesac.. 35
  Unleavened Bread, Hag HaMatzeh 41
  First Fruits, of the Barley Harvest 50
  Pentecost, Weeks 54

Latter Rain (fall) Festivals 63
  The Return, Teshuvah................................. 64
  Trumpets, Rosh Hashanah 69
  Days of Awe, Yamin Noraim 84
  Day of Atonement, Yom Kippur 95
  Tabernacles, Sukkot................................... 104
  The Great Salvation, The Great Day 116
  The Eighth Conclusion, Shimini Atzeret........ 121

Other Prophetic Ceremonies 125
  Hanukkah... 126
  New Moon.. 129
  Ninth of Av, Tisha B'Av 133
  Purim 138
  Red Heifer.. 140
  Wedding Ceremony 144

Tribulation Period Outline 149
  The First 3.5 Years 150
  The Second 3.5 Years 154

Appendices 157
  Appendix A Halloween 158
  Appendix B Types and Shadows Charts 161

Other Books by Ken Johnson, Th.D. 163
Bibliography 169

Introduction

In AD 2008 we published *Ancient Prophecies Revealed*, which gave many of the regular prophecies in chronological order. Fifty-four have been fulfilled since Israel became a state in AD 1948. There is another type of prophecy that is wrapped up in the symbolism and timing of the Jewish temple rituals: the ancient messianic festivals.

In Leviticus 23 God gave seven festivals for the Jews to observe. Buried deep within the rituals performed on these holy days are types and shadows that predict events that would occur during the first and second comings of the Messiah.

> These *are* the feasts of the LORD, *even* holy convocations, which ye shall proclaim in their seasons... Speak unto the children of Israel, saying, In the seventh month, in the first *day* of the month, shall ye have a sabbath, a memorial of blowing of trumpets, an holy convocation. *Leviticus 23:4, 24*

The festivals are given in Leviticus 23 and Numbers 28-29. The Hebrew word for "festivals" is *hagim*, which means a yearly recurring event. The Hebrew words for "holy convocation" are *mikra kodesh*. *Kodesh* is the Hebrew word for holy or sanctified. The word *mikra* has two meanings: first, a required assembly and second, a recital. This implies that the rituals preformed on these festivals predict what God will do in the future. The Hebrew word for "feasts" and "appointed times" is *moedim*, which means an appointment. Notice that these are also called Sabbaths even though they may fall on any day of the week. The Hebrew word here for "sabbaths" is *shabaton,* meaning a high Sabbath. There are seven shabaton that occur during the year.

These seven shabaton teach that God's people have an appointment to gather together at a specific place at a special time and perform a specific ritual. It also shows that the Messiah will appear on those special dates in those special places in some future year and accomplish what the ritual predicts.

The apostle Paul refers to these rituals as types and shadows. They are a symbolic form of prophecy.

> Let no man therefore judge you in meat, or in drink, or in respect of an holyday, or of the new moon, or of the sabbath *days:* which are a shadow of things to come; but the body *is* of Christ. *Colossians 2:16-17*

It is our purpose to reveal the hidden meanings of these rituals so that every Christian can be equipped to fully understand prophecy. The believers in Thessalonica were Gentiles, but they still understood that the Hebrew festivals taught about the first and second comings of the Messiah. Paul said;

> But of the times and the seasons, brethren, ye have no need that I write unto you. *1 Thessalonians 5:1*

Paul is speaking of the times *moedim* that occur in their proper seasons (former and latter rain).

The Bible provides most of the information on the rituals and sacrifices. About 200 A.D. the Mishnah was written under the direction of Judah HaNasi. The Mishnah is the oral Torah, or the details of each part of the rituals and the comments of the rabbis on those subjects. We will build our understanding about the festivals from the Scriptures, then see if the teachings of the ancient rabbis shed any more light on the meaning of the rituals.

Note that observance of these festivals and other Jewish rituals are not binding on the church of God. In Acts 15, when questions were raised about gentile believers observing the Sabbath, circumcision, and the festivals, the apostles wrote a letter to all the gentile churches stating that these were not necessary for them to observe. If they refrained from idolatry, fornication, and the eating of blood, they would do well.

It is perfectly permissible for a Gentile to observe all or part of the festivals and it is important that all believers understand the types and shadows in the festival rituals. The apostle Paul stated we are not to allow anyone to judge us whether we observe the rituals or not.

> Let no man therefore judge you in meat, or in drink, or in respect of an holyday, or of the new moon, or of the sabbath *days:* Which are a shadow of things to come; but the body *is* of Christ. *Colossians 2:16-17*

The Jewish Calendars

To accurately find the dates of the festivals we need to know a few things about the biblical calendar.

The Day

In the modern American calendar our day begins at 12:00 AM, midnight, and ends the following midnight. This twenty-four-hour period is one day or one day and night. In Genesis 1, we see that the Hebrew day is calculated on a different basis: "the evening and the morning," not from midnight to midnight.

> And God called the light Day, and the darkness He called Night. And the evening and the morning were the first day. *Genesis 1:5*

The Hebrew day begins at sunset and continues though the morning to the next sunset. In the following example the second day of the Jewish month,

Tishrei	
Sunday	Monday
1	2

Tishrei, is Monday. We are to understand, in this case, that the second of Tishrei begins on Sunday at sunset and ends on Monday at sunset. The majority of the day occurs on Monday, so that is where the second is placed on the calendar, but instead of starting at 12:00 AM, the Jewish day starts about six hours earlier.

The Month

The Genesis record shows Noah's flood started on the seventeenth day of the second month and ended on the seventeenth day of the seventh month. This period lasted 150 days, which means each month consisted of thirty days each. The prophetic calendar is based on twelve, thirty-day months – or a total of 360 days per year.

In the six hundredth year of Noah's life, in the second month, the seventeenth day of the month, the same day were all the fountains of the great deep broken up, and the windows of heaven were opened.
Genesis 7:11

And the waters returned from off the earth continually: and after the end of the hundred and fifty days the waters were abated. And the ark rested in the seventh month, on the seventeenth day of the month, upon the mountains of Ararat. *Genesis 8:3-4*

It has been theorized that the year actually consisted of 360 days until the time of Noah's Flood. With the Flood's destruction the rotation of the earth was changed so that we now have 365.25 days per year.

Spring and Fall Equinox
Modern Jewish calendar rules ensure that Yom Kippur and Hoshana Rabbah do not fall on a Friday (Sabbath). This is done simply by switching days in the previous months to ensure Rosh Hashanah does not fall on a Sunday, Wednesday, or Friday. Current rabbinical thought is that if these high holy days fell on a Sabbath, the Sabbath rules would prevent orthodox Jews from performing the rituals needed that year.

Anciently this was not so. The rabbis would go out each night to observe the moon phase. On the night when the slightest sliver of the moon was seen, the shofar was blown declaring the new month had begun. Each month always began on a new moon. Most festivals occur around the middle of the month, on the 15th or full moon.

Ancient Messianic Festivals

The easiest way to verify when the real festivals and future prophecies will occur is to memorize the dates of the spring and fall equinoxes. Spring begins between March 20 and March 22, the spring equinox. Fall begins between September 20 and September 22, or the fall or autumnal equinox. The first new moon following the spring equinox is the first of Nisan. The first new moon following the fall equinox will be the first of Tishri.

Several eminent Israeli archeologists like Yigdal Yadin have suggested the Essenes of Qumran had one of the more accurate calendar systems. Their calendar was based on the solar year with twelve months of thirty days each, with one intercalary day after every three months. This is similar to the calendar system used in the Dead Sea Scroll, the *Book of Jubilees*.

The Year
Throughout the year the festivals that God ordained are commemorated on the date prescribed in Scripture. We will notice that there are patterns to some dates not mentioned in Scripture.

Festival Dates

Festival	Jewish Date	Occurs in
Purim	Adar 14-15	Feb.-Mar.
Passover	Nisan 14	Mar.-Apr.
Unleavened Bread	Nisan 15-21	
First Fruits (Barley)	The Sunday after Passover	
Pentecost (Weeks)	Sivan 6	May-June
Rosh Hashanah	Tishrei 1-2	Sept.-Oct.
Yom Kippur	Tishrei 10	Sept.-Oct.
Tabernacles	Tishrei 15-21	Sept.-Oct.
Hoshana Rabbah	Tishrei 21	Sept.-Oct.
Shimini Azteret	Tishrei 22	Sept.-Oct.
Jeroboam's Festival	Heshvan 15	Oct.-Nov.
Hanukkah	Kislev 25	Nov.-Dec.

The Two Jewish Calendars

To make things more complicated, we discover that there are two Jewish calendars found in the Bible. The original civil calendar starts in the month of Tishrei (in the fall). We see it exclusively from Genesis to Exodus 12.

When God gave Moses the Law at Mount Sinai, He commanded a religious calendar to be observed. The sacred calendar starts in the month of Nisan, also called Abib (in the spring). From this point onward secular events are recorded on the civil calendar and religious events are recorded on the sacred calendar. The civil calendar is the standard one used by Jews today. This is why the Jewish New Year takes place in the fall.

> This month *shall be* unto you the beginning of months: it *shall be* the first month of the year to you...
> This day came ye out in the month Abib.
> *Exodus 12:2; 13:4*

We will see that the Messiah died on the 14th of Nisan and resurrected on Sunday, the 17th of Nisan. However, on the modern calendar the 17th of Nisan never falls on a Sunday, because of these new calendar rules.

The Two Jewish Calendars

Month	Corresponds with	Days	Civil	Sacred
Tishrei	Sept-Oct.	30 days	1st	7th
Heshvan	Oct-Nov.	29 or 30	2nd	8th
Kislev	Nov-Dec.	29 or 30	3rd	9th
Teveth	Dec-Jan.	29	4th	10th
Shvat	Jan-Feb.	30	5th	11th
Adar	Feb-Mar	29 or 30	6th	12th
Nisan/Abib	Mar-Apr	30	7th	1st
Iyar	Apr-May	29	8th	2nd
Sivan	May-June	30	9th	3rd
Tammuz	June-July	29	10th	4th
Av	July-Aug.	30	11th	5th
Elul	Aug.-Sept.	29	12th	6th

There are two modern Jewish calendars; the civil calendar that starts in the fall and the sacred calendar that starts in the spring. Modern calendar rules manipulate the days of the month, change them from thirty to twenty-nine or vise versa, to ensure Yom Kippur does not fall on a Sabbath.

The Former and Latter Rain

The springtime rainy season is often referred to as the season of the former rains, while the autumn rainy season can be referred to as the season of the latter rains. The prophet Hosea described the Messiah's First Coming, when He died for us, as occurring in the spring (former rain) and His Second Coming, when He will establish the messianic kingdom, as occurring in the fall (latter rain).

> Then shall we know, *if* we follow on to know the LORD: His going forth is prepared as the morning; and He shall come unto us as the rain, as the latter *and* former rain unto the earth. *Hosea 6:3*

James directly interprets Hosea's reference as referring to the comings of our Lord.

> Be patient therefore, brethren, unto the coming of the Lord. Behold, the husbandman waiteth for the precious fruit of the earth, and hath long patience for it, until he receive the early and latter rain. *James 5:7*

The prophet Joel writes that the Teacher of Righteousness will come like the former and latter rains "in the first month."

> Be glad then, ye children of Zion, and rejoice in the LORD your God: for He hath given you the <u>former rain moderately</u>, and He will cause to come down for you the rain, the former rain, and the latter rain in the first *month. Joel 2:23*

Ancient Messianic Festivals

The Hebrew word מורה, *moreh*, translated "former rain" in the KJV can mean teacher or early rain. The Hebrew word צדקה, *zedekah*, can mean righteousness or moderation. Joel is stating the first coming of the Messiah would occur in the first month of the spring calendar, which is the month of Nisan or Abib, and that the Messiah's second coming will occur in the first month of the fall calendar, or Tishri.

The following chart shows the spring and fall festivals. In the succeeding chapters we will look in detail at the rituals performed on these festivals and see what God has to tell us about the comings of the Messiah.

The Two Sets of Festivals

Spring - Nisan The First Coming	Fall - Tishri The Second Coming
Passover Unleavened Bread First Fruits (Barley) Weeks (Pentecost)	Rosh Hashanah Day of Atonement Tabernacles

In Romans, Paul stated that the temple services were given by God and are "without repentance." They are without repentance because they are promises or prophecies in themselves.

> Who are Israelites; to whom *pertaineth* the adoption, and the glory, and the covenants, and the giving of the law, and the service *of God,* and the promises; whose *are* the fathers, and of whom as concerning the flesh Christ *came,* who is over all, God blessed for ever. Amen. *Romans 9:4-5*

For the gifts and calling of God *are* without repentance. *Romans 11:29*

The temple services are the promises, or prophecies, described in Leviticus 23 and Numbers 28-29.

Weekly Sabbath

Six days shall work be done: but the seventh day *is* the sabbath of rest, an holy convocation; ye shall do no work *therein:* it *is* the sabbath of the LORD in all your dwellings. *Leviticus 23:3*

Passover

These *are* the feasts of the LORD, *even* holy convocations, which ye shall proclaim in their seasons. In the fourteenth *day* of the first month at even *is* the LORD'S passover. *Leviticus 23:4-5*

Unleavened Bread

And on the fifteenth day of the same month *is* the feast of unleavened bread unto the LORD: seven days ye must eat unleavened bread. In the first day ye shall have an holy convocation: ye shall do no servile work therein. But ye shall offer an offering made by fire unto the LORD seven days: in the seventh day *is* a holy convocation: ye shall do no servile work *therein.* *Leviticus 23:6-8*

First Fruits

Speak unto the children of Israel, and say unto them, When ye be come into the land which I give unto you, and shall reap the harvest thereof, then ye shall bring a sheaf of the first fruits of your harvest unto the priest: and he shall wave the sheaf before the LORD, to be accepted for you: on the morrow after the sabbath the priest shall wave it. *Leviticus 23:10-11*

Pentecost

And ye shall count unto you from the morrow after the sabbath, from the day that ye brought the sheaf of the wave offering; seven sabbaths shall be complete: even unto the morrow after the seventh sabbath shall ye number fifty days; and ye shall offer a new meat offering unto the LORD... And ye shall proclaim on the selfsame day, *that* it may be a holy convocation unto you: ye shall do no servile work *therein: it shall be* a statute for ever in all your dwellings throughout your generations. *Leviticus 23:15-16,21*

Trumpets

Speak unto the children of Israel, saying, In the seventh month, in the first *day* of the month, shall ye have a sabbath, a memorial of blowing of trumpets, a holy convocation. Ye shall do no servile work *therein:* but ye shall offer an offering made by fire unto the LORD. *Leviticus 23:24-25*

Atonement

Also on the tenth *day* of this seventh month *there shall be* a day of atonement: it shall be a holy convocation unto you; and ye shall afflict your souls, and offer an offering made by fire unto the LORD. And ye shall do no work in that same day: for it *is* a day of atonement, to make an atonement for you before the LORD your God. *Leviticus 23:27-28*

Tabernacles

Speak unto the children of Israel, saying, The fifteenth day of this seventh month *shall be* the feast of tabernacles *for* seven days unto the LORD. On the first day *shall be* a holy convocation: ye shall do no servile work *therein. Leviticus 23:34-35*

Eighth Day
Seven days ye shall offer an offering made by fire unto the LORD: on the eighth day shall be a holy convocation unto you; and ye shall offer an offering made by fire unto the LORD: it *is* a solemn assembly; *and* ye shall do no servile work *therein.* *Leviticus 23:36*

On the eighth day ye shall have a solemn assembly: ye shall do no servile work *therein: Numbers 29:35*

Seven Festivals and their Parts
The seven festivals are Passover, Unleavened Bread, First Fruits, Pentecost, Trumpets, Atonement, and Tabernacles. Some of these festivals have multiple parts. Passover has *Bedhot Chamits*, or the Search for the Leaven. Trumpets has the Days of Awe and *Teshuvah*. Tabernacles has the Great Day, the Eighth Day, and the Rejoicing in the Torah.

Encyclopedia Judaica
As we go though the festivals, I would encourage you to look up each of the titles for each of the festivals in the Encyclopedia Judaica and other ancient Jewish works to not only verify what I am teaching, but to learn even more for your own personal study and witness for the Lord.

Weekly Sabbath, Shabbat

שבת

God gave Moses the ritual for the keeping of the Sabbath. This consisted of two parts: the general Sabbath ritual which was performed at the beginning of the Sabbath, Friday night, and the *Havdala* ritual which was performed at the end of the Sabbath, or Saturday night.

The Rabbis

Many of the ancient rabbis pondered why God would create everything over a period of six days, then rest on a seventh day, when He could have created everything in a split second. When they came to Psalm 90:4, written by Moses, they concluded God was going to allow six thousand years for human history to occur, then create a thousand-year messianic kingdom.

Thus the heavens and the earth were finished, and all the host of them. And on the seventh day God ended His work which He had made; and He rested on the seventh day from all His work which He had made. And God blessed the seventh day, and sanctified it: because that in it He had rested from all His work which God created and made. *Genesis 2:1-3*

For a thousand years in thy sight *are but* as yesterday when it is past, and *as* a watch in the night. *Psalms 90:4*

The rabbis called this present age the *Olam HaZeh* and the coming age the *Olam HaBa*.

The Apostles

In Matthew 24:3, when the disciples asked what were the signs of the "end of the age" they were referring to the Olam HaZeh. Paul used this same phrase, Olam HaZeh, when he taught that Jesus delivered us from this "present world" in Galatians 1:4; and that Demas left him for the love of this "present world" in 2 Timothy 4:10; and we should avoid the sins of this "present age" in Titus 2:12. Jesus' future kingdom is mentioned as the "world to come" in Ephesians 1:21; Hebrews 2:5; and 6:5. The thousand-year reign of Christ is directly taught in Revelation 20; and Peter alluded to Psalm 90:4 when speaking of the coming destruction and messianic kingdom.

But, beloved, be not ignorant of this one thing, that one day *is* with the Lord as a thousand years, and a thousand years as one day. The Lord is not slack concerning his promise, as some men count slackness; but is longsuffering to us-ward, not willing that any should perish, but that all should come to repentance. But the day of the Lord will come as a thief in the night; in the which the heavens shall pass away with a great noise, and the elements shall melt with fervent heat, the earth also and the works that are therein shall be burned up. *2 Peter 3:8-10*

... and they lived and reigned with Christ a thousand years. *Revelation 20:4*

Many of the ancient church fathers looked at these verses and taught the Second Coming would occur in the year 6,000 AM. AM stands for Anno Mundi meaning "in the year of the world." With the calendars being confused and inaccurate, we can't say for certain when the year 6,000 will occur. An approximate range would be between the years AD 2030 and 2070, although it could occur even earlier. See *Ancient Post-Flood History* for more information on the historical timeline.

The Ancient Church Fathers

The idea that Jesus will return to set up His millennial kingdom in the Jewish year 6,000 is taught by several ancient church fathers. The First Coming of Jesus Christ was about 4,000 years after Creation. These ancient church fathers taught the Second Coming would be about AD 2000. The most descriptive explanation is in the Epistle of Barnabas which devotes an entire chapter to this issue. Remember, this does not mean they were correct; but it shows how they perceived the typological prophecy of the Sabbath. Here are a few quotes on the issue.

Barnabas, AD 100

Epistle of Barnabas 15:7-9 – Therefore, children, in six days, or in six thousand years, all the prophecies will be fulfilled. Then it says, He rested on the seventh day. This signifies at the Second Coming of our Lord Jesus, He will destroy the Antichrist, judge the ungodly, and change the sun, moon, and stars. Then He will truly rest during the millennial reign, which is the seventh day.

Irenaeus, AD 180

Against Heresies 5.28 – The day of the Lord is as a thousand years; and in six days created things were completed. It is evident, therefore, they will come to an end in the six thousandth year.

Hippolytus, AD 205

Fragment 2; Commentary on Daniel 2.4 – The Sabbath is a type of the future kingdom... For "a day with the Lord is as a thousand years." Since, then, in six days the Lord created all things, it follows that in six thousand years all will be fulfilled.

Commodianus, AD 240

Against the Gods of the Heathens 35 – We will be immortal when the six thousand years are completed.

Against the Gods of the Heathens 80 – Resurrection of the body will be when six thousand years are completed, and after the one thousand years [millennial reign], the world will come to an end.

Victorinus, AD 240

Commentary on Revelation 20.1-3 – Satan will be bound until the thousand years are finished. That is, after the sixth day.

Methodius, AD 290

Ten Virgins 9.1 – In the seventh millennium we will be immortal and truly celebrate the Feast of Tabernacles.

Lactantius, AD 304

Divine Institutes 7.14 – The sixth thousandth year is not yet complete. When this number is complete, the consummation must take place.

Observing the Sabbath and Festivals Not Necessary

Acts 15 clearly taught that Christians are not required to keep any of the rituals Moses passed down. Paul even stated in Colossians 2:16-17 we are not to let anyone judge us whether we keep the seven festivals and the weekly Sabbath or not. However, all wise Christians take the time to understand the true meaning of the rituals. One ancient Dead Sea Scroll puts it this way:

> The Creator blessed it [the seventh day]; but He did not sanctify all nations and all peoples to observe the Sabbath on it, only Israel alone. *Jubilees 2*

The ancient church fathers taught the meaning of the rituals in depth, but stated the observance of them was not needed.

Mathetes, AD 130
Epistle to Diognetus 3, 4 – Christians do not offer sacrifices, abstain from meats, observe the Sabbath or new moon festivals like the Jews do.

Justin Martyr, AD 165
Dialogue 19 to 23 – Circumcision, food laws, and Sabbaths were for a teaching. Circumcision began with Abraham and the Sabbath and the rest began with Moses.

Dialogue 43 – Circumcision began with Abraham. The Sabbath, sacrifices, offerings, and feasts began with Moses.

First Apology 67 – Christians meet together on Sunday.

Dialogue 10 – Christians live like all other Gentiles, not observing the festivals, Sabbaths, new moon, or the rite of circumcision.

Ignatius, AD 30 - 107
Trallians 9 – Christians do not observe the Sabbath but the Lord's Day.

Irenaeus, 177 AD
Against Heresies 4.4 – The Law started with Moses and ended with John [the Baptist].

Against Heresies 4.16 – Men were never released from the Decalogue. We, however, do not observe the Sabbath, or circumcision.

Against Heresies 4.34 – Jesus fulfilled the law and prophets, then did away with it, and gave a new covenant.

Against Heresies 5.8 – In the dispensation of Law, the clean animals represented spiritual man and the unclean animals represented the carnal man.

Tertullian, AD 210

Marcion 4.12 – Jesus annulled the Sabbath.

Jews 1.3 – Circumcision was temporary.

Jews 1.4 – Sabbath was temporary.

Jews 1.5 – Sacrifices were temporary.

The Year 6000

We can see from these quotes that many of the ancient rabbis and ancient church fathers believed the Second Coming would be 6000 years after creation. The Jewish calendar began at creation. So it would be the Jewish year 6000 AM. As we said, AM stands for Anno Mundi meaning "in the year of the world." The modern Gregorian calendar dates from the time of Christ. It is abbreviated AD which stands for Anno Domini, meaning "in the year of our Lord."

The current Jewish year corresponding to our AD 2012 is 5772 AM. If this is correct, then creation was 5,772 years ago. The Babylonian Talmud is the modern source for Jewish history. Comparing it to the Bible and the book of Jasher, it is accurate up to the time of the Persian rule. The Talmud often quotes an ancient Jewish history book called the Seder Olam. It is highly accurate up until the time of the Persians, but tells the story of a rabbi named Yose, who deliberately changed the calendar because too many people realized the prophecy of Daniel 9 accurately predicted the time of the Messiah's death to be April 6, AD 32. He wanted to change it so Daniel's date could mean from the destruction of the first temple to the destruction of the second temple. So he taught that Cyrus, Darius, and Xerxes were titles for the same person, thus condensing the Persian rule from 210 years to only 24 years. See *Ancient Seder Olam* for full details. Bishop Ussher calculated the date of Creation to be 4004 BC. In the book *Ancient Post-Flood History*, the dates are calculated based on the Bible, the *Ancient Seder Olam*, and the *Ancient Book of Jasher,* placing the destruction of Solomon's temple on 3338 AM. All modern historians place the destruction of Solomon's Temple at 586/587 BC. This would place Creation at 3924/3925 BC.

We cannot be certain of the modern date for 6000 AM, but it should be somewhere between AD 2030 and AD 2070.

The Tribulation
At the beginning of the Sabbath the priests cleanse the temple, wash down the altar, and take the ashes out of the temple to a valley called Motzah. Since the ancient church fathers taught the Sabbath is a picture of the millennial reign, they reasoned that this procedure of cleansing the altar before the start of the Sabbath teaches that the Tribulation, or cleansing of the earth, occurs prior to the Millennium.

Havdalah
At the end of every Sabbath and festival there is a ritual called the *Havdalah*. It closes out the holy time and prepares to return the worshipers to the world of the mundane.

A Havdalah candle is a special candle made up of three separate candles braided together. It is called the torch[a], or *lapidot* in Hebrew. It symbolizes the Messiah as the light of the world and also pictures the trinity. In the Havdalah service those present form a circle. The priest circles the congregants, carrying the torch close enough to each person's hand for them to feel the heat.

In some messianic congregations, Habakkuk 3:4 is read as each person raises his hands in the cohanim blessing (shown on the next page).

His brightness was like the light; He had rays flashing from His hand, and there His power was hidden. *Habakkuk 3:4 NKJV*

This blessing teaches that the Messiah's power to save us comes from the crucifixion, as graphically displayed by the light passing though each person's fingers. Today, this reminds us of the wounds in Messiah's hands from the crucifixion.

Following the passing of the torch, the *Hamadvil* prayer is lifted up.

Elijah the prophet, Elijah the Tishbite, Elijah the Giladite, may he arrive quickly in our time with the Messiah, son of David. May He who separates between the sacred and the everyday forgive our sins; may He multiply our offspring and our money like the sand, and like the stars at night. A good week! *Hamadvil*

---

[a] See also Genesis 15:17

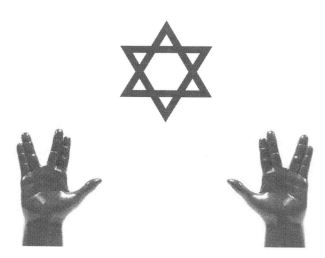

This symbol for the priestly blessing is found on all arks today (the cabinet that houses the Torah scroll in the back of a synagogue).

In this prayer, which originally was part of the *Neilah* or concluding service, the worshipper once again acknowledges that God has set the Sabbath apart and prepares to enter the week.

Once the songs and prayers are done, the Havdalah candle is lifted up for all to see and then extinguished in the cup of wine symbolizing the death of the Messiah by His shedding of blood. The room goes entirely dark even as the world is dark without the light of the Torch, the Messiah.

At this point the Sabbath has officially ended and each individual lights their own candle. This is the setting for Acts 20 where the believers have gathered together for a Havdalah.

And upon the first *day* of the week, when the disciples came together to break bread, Paul preached unto them, ready to depart on the morrow; and continued his speech until midnight. And there were many lights in the upper chamber, where they were gathered together. *Acts 20:7-8*

The Havdalah service teaches us that the Messiah came and fulfilled the prophecies of the former rain. We are now separated, awaiting His return to fulfill the latter rain prophecies.

Ancient Messianic Festivals

Former Rain (spring) Festivals

1. Passover
   Bedhot Chamits
2. Unleavened Bread
3. First Fruits
4. Pentecost

Search for the Leaven, Bedhot Chamets

בדהת חמץ

Adar						
S	M	T	W	T	F	S
			1	2	3	4
5	6	7	8	9	10	11
12	13	14	15	16	17	18
19	20	21	22	23	24	25
26	27	28	29	30		

Nissan						
S	M	T	W	T	F	S
					1	2
3	4	5	6	7	8	9
10	11	12	13	14	15	16
17	18	19	20	21	22	23
24	25	26	27	28	29	30

For one month prior to Passover the mother of the home does a thorough cleaning. She makes sure there is no leaven (chamets) in the house anywhere. She will clean from Adar 15 to Nisan 14.

The evening before the day of the fourteenth (preparation day, when the Passover lamb is slain) the ceremony called *Bedhot Chamets*, the search for the leaven, is conducted in the home by the father.

The mother purposely left ten pieces of leaven somewhere in the house. The father knows where they are. The father gathers the family together and presents to them a candle, a wooden spoon, a feather, and a linen cloth. They then wait until dark. The father begins the ritual by reading Zephaniah 1:12.

And it shall come to pass at that time, *that* I will search Jerusalem with candles, and punish the men that are settled on their lees: that say in their heart, The LORD will not do good, neither will He do evil. *Zephaniah 1:12*

The family searches the house with the candle. When the leaven pieces are found, the father places the wooden spoon next to them and sweeps the leaven into the spoon with the feather. When all ten pieces are collected, they are wrapped in the linen cloth together with the spoon and feather. Then the father goes to the door of the home and casts out the leaven. He then declares "If there be any leaven, let it be null and void."

The next morning (the day of Nissan 14) the father goes out, picks up the bundle, and takes it to the local synagogue and burns it there in a special fire created for this ceremony.

The symbolism is clear. The leaven represents sin; the wooden spoon, the cross; the feather, the Holy Spirit; the linen cloth, the burial shroud of Christ.

John 2:13-17 records that Jesus went into the temple when Passover was at hand and cleansed the temple. Jesus was fulfilling the Bedhot Chamets!

The Apostle Paul used this ritual to teach that we must, through the power of the Holy Spirit, purge sin out of our lives.

> Purge out therefore the old leaven, that ye may be a new lump, as ye are unleavened. For even Christ our passover is sacrificed for us: therefore let us keep the feast, not with old leaven, neither with the leaven of malice and wickedness; but with the unleavened *bread* of sincerity and truth. *1 Corinthians 5:7-8*

Using the calendar at the beginning of this chapter, Bedhot Chamets would have been performed on Wednesday night and the old leaven burned on Thursday morning. The rest of Thursday until 6 PM is used to prepare for the festival of Unleavened Bread. This day is called Passover.

Passover,
Pesac

פסכ

Nissan						
S	M	T	W	T	F	S
					1	2
3	4	5	6	7	8	9
10	11	12	13	14	15	16
17	18	19	20	21	22	23
24	25	26	27	28	29	30

The Passover commemorates the children of Israel leaving Egypt in the Exodus under Moses. The ritual demonstrates the coming Messiah's death, burial, and resurrection.

And in the fourteenth day of the first month *is* the passover of the LORD. And in the fifteenth day of this month *is* the feast: seven days shall unleavened bread be eaten. In the first day *shall be* an holy convocation; ye shall do no manner of servile work *therein: Numbers 28:16-18*

Historical
The Passover historically commemorates the time when God delivered the Children of Israel from slavery in Egypt. God swore to Abraham that after 430 years He would bring his descendants into the land of Canaan and make them a great nation (Genesis 15). This occurred 430

later, to the very day (Exodus 12:41, Galatians 3:16-17). This was the year 2448 AM on the Jewish calendar, which is approximately 1450 BC.

> And it came to pass at the end of the four hundred and thirty years, even the selfsame day it came to pass, that all the hosts of the LORD went out from the land of Egypt. *Exodus 12:41*

As commanded, they prepared the lamb and Passover meal on the fourteenth of Nisan. That night (on the fifteenth) they ate the Passover meal and performed the rituals as commanded, dressed for their departure, and made ready to go.

The death angel came and destroyed any firstborn not protected by the blood on the doorposts; and by midnight the decree came from Pharaoh to let the Israelites go. They then left Egypt shortly after midnight.

The Israelites killed a lamb on the fourteenth (cooking must be done by 6 PM), ate the lamb, and left Egypt on the fifteenth (Seder must be done by 12 AM). They crossed the Red Sea on the seventeenth.

Preparation for the Passover - Nisan 14
According to the Mishnah, *Moed* (set feasts), *Pesahim* (Passover), the father of the house would go choose a lamb without spot or blemish on the tenth of Nisan and take it home. For four days all could inspect the lamb to guarantee it was truly perfect. Then on the fourteenth of Nisan at the time called "between the evenings," or 3 PM, the father would bring the family outside of the house and place the lamb in the doorway of the house and kill it. He gathered the blood in a basin placed in the threshold of the doorway. The father then put his family back inside

the house and took hyssop and dipped it in the blood and used it to place the lamb's blood on the lintel and the two door posts. The blood then formed a pattern of a cross on the door, when it dripped down to the threshold.

The lamb was then skinned and roasted upright on a pomegranate stick with a cross piece to hold it open. The intestines were prepared and placed around the head to be roasted also. This was called "the crowned sacrifice." So we see the lamb on a cross with a crown on its head!

The mother and father must finish cooking the lamb before the evening. That evening as dusk turns into the 15th of Nisan (which is a high Sabbath[b]), the Passover Seder meal begins.

The Temple Ritual
In the time of Jesus, the high priest, on the 10th of Nisan, would go to Bethany to choose an unblemished lamb and bring it into the temple to be inspected for four days. As the lamb was brought to the Eastern Gate, pilgrims would line the sides of the road leading to the gate and wave the palm branches and say "Baruch Ha Shem Adonai," which means "blessed is he who comes in the name of the Lord," quoted from Psalm 118:26-27. At 9 AM on the fourteenth of Nisan, the lamb was tied to one of the horns of the altar. At 3 PM, the high priest would slay the lamb while saying the words "it is finished." These specific words are spoken at any "shelem" or peace offering.

How Jesus Fulfilled the Passover
The temple ritual teaches us about the Messiah's death. Jesus left the house of Lazarus in Bethany on Nissan 10 to

---

[b] A high Sabbath is one of the seven Festivals, while a regular or low Sabbath is the weekly Sabbath.

teach in the Temple. There the scribes asked their hardest questions of Jesus and walked away saying "never a man spoke as this man." So Jesus was without blemish. Jesus was hung on the cross at 9 AM and died at 3:00 PM, or "between the evenings" on Nissan 14. He acted as both priest and sacrifice when He said, "it is finished," and then died.

John the Baptist believed that the Passover lamb prophetically typified Jesus when he said:

> The next day John seeth Jesus coming unto him, and saith, Behold the Lamb of God, which taketh away the sin of the world. *John 1:29*

Jesus said Jerusalem would be destroyed because the Jews did not truly believe the prophecies that told of the time of His coming and the rituals in the temple that described Him. Exactly forty years *to the day* after Jesus gave this prophecy, the Roman general Titus destroyed the temple.

> "And shall lay thee even with the ground, and thy children within thee; and they shall not leave in thee one stone upon another; because thou knewest not the time of thy visitation." *Luke 19:44*

Jesus died on Thursday, Nisan 14, the "preparation day" and Joseph of Arimathea placed Jesus in a tomb before 6 PM.

> The Jews therefore, because it was the preparation, that the bodies should not remain upon the cross on the sabbath day, (for that sabbath day was an high day,) besought Pilate that their legs might be broken, and *that* they might be taken away. *John 19:31*

And now when the even was come, because it was the preparation, that is, the day before the sabbath, Joseph of Arimathaea, an honourable counsellor, which also waited for the kingdom of God, came, and went in boldly unto Pilate, and craved the body of Jesus. *Mark 15:42-43*

Jesus was in the grave for three days and three nights until His resurrection on Sunday, Nisan 17.

Then certain of the scribes and of the Pharisees answered, saying, Master, we would see a sign from thee. But He answered and said unto them, An evil and adulterous generation seeketh after a sign; and there shall no sign be given to it, but the sign of the prophet Jonas: for as Jonas was three days and three nights in the whale's belly; so shall the Son of man be three days and three nights in the heart of the earth. *Matthew 12:38-40*

A Note about Prophecy
Anyone who really believes the prophecies would have known the exact day of the Exodus, because of the 430-year-prophecy God gave to Abraham. Likewise, they would have known the exact time of the crucifixion of the Messiah based on Daniel's 70-Weeks prophecy.

And it came to pass at the end of the four hundred and thirty years, even the selfsame day it came to pass, that all the hosts of the LORD went out from the land of Egypt. *Exodus 12:41*

The Second Coming prophecies are just as accurate!

Ancient Messianic Festivals

Biblical events that occurred on Nisan 10
Took an unspotted lamb home
Jesus showed himself in the temple
God commanded Abraham to travel to Mt. Moriah to sacrifice Isaac
Passover lamb put on display in the Temple

Biblical events that occurred on Nisan 14
The unspotted lamb is slain at 3 PM
Jesus died at 3 PM
Isaac was born
Abraham sacrificed a ram on Mt. Moriah in place of Isaac
The Exodus from Egypt occurred
Fall of Masada occurred

Unleavened Bread, Hag HaMatzeh

הג המצה

Nissan						
S	M	T	W	T	F	S
					1	2
3	4	5	6	7	8	9
10	11	12	13	14	15	16
17	18	19	20	21	22	23
24	25	26	27	28	29	30

The festival of Unleavened Bread is a seven day festival that occurs on Nisan 15-21. The Song of Solomon is read during the festival of *Hag Ha Matzeh*.

In the fourteenth *day* of the first month at even *is* the LORD'S passover. And on the fifteenth day of the same month *is* the feast of unleavened bread unto the LORD: seven days ye must eat unleavened bread. In the first day ye shall have an holy convocation: ye shall do no servile work therein. *Leviticus 23:5-7*

The Lamb prepared on the 14th, (preparation day) is now eaten in a ritual meal called the *Seder*. Seder means "set order."

This month *shall be* unto you the beginning of months: it *shall be* the first month of the year to you.

Speak ye unto all the congregation of Israel, saying, In the tenth *day* of this month they shall take to them every man a lamb, according to the house of *their* fathers, a lamb for an house: and if the household be too little for the lamb, let him and his neighbour next unto his house take *it* according to the number of the souls; every man according to his eating shall make your count for the lamb. Your lamb shall be without blemish, a male of the first year: ye shall take *it* out from the sheep, or from the goats: and ye shall keep it up until the fourteenth day of the same month: and the whole assembly of the congregation of Israel shall kill it in the evening. And they shall take of the blood, and strike *it* on the two side posts and on the upper door post of the houses, wherein they shall eat it. And they shall eat the flesh in that night, roast with fire, and unleavened bread; *and* with bitter *herbs* they shall eat it. Eat not of it raw, nor sodden at all with water, but roast *with* fire; his head with his legs, and with the purtenance thereof. And ye shall let nothing of it remain until the morning; and that which remaineth of it until the morning ye shall burn with fire. And thus shall ye eat it; *with* your loins girded, your shoes on your feet, and your staff in your hand; and ye shall eat it in haste: it *is* the LORD'S passover.
Exodus 12:2-11

The Seder
The Passover Seder is the ritual that families observe at home. It commemorates the Exodus from Egypt, but it also teaches about the coming of the Messiah. The Seder starts at 6 PM and must be finished by 12 AM. On the dining table is a special cloth container with three pockets called a *Matzah-Tash* with a loaf of unleavened bread in each pocket. This symbolizes the Trinity. The middle loaf of unleavened bread, or Matzah, is taken out and torn in

two. The smaller piece is placed back in the pocket between the other two. The father of the household wraps the larger piece in a napkin and hides it somewhere in the house. This symbolizes the death and burial of the second person of the Trinity, the Son. It will be used later for the *Afikomen*. Then the story of the Exodus from Egypt is told, and the group sings Psalms 113-114. Next, the father brings out the lower peace of Matzah from the Matzah-Tash, blesses it, and each member eats a small piece of the bread. This symbolizes the Holy Spirit, third person of the Trinity. Finally, the Passover meal is eaten, which may take several hours.

After the meal, the father sends the children to search for the hidden Matzah. The Seder cannot continue until the Matzah is found and given back to the father. This symbolizes the resurrection and ascension of the Messiah. The child negotiates what gift the father will give him for returning the Matzah. Then the father gives the child a coin as a down payment for the gift, the Matzah is returned, and the Seder can continue. This gift of a coin is referred to as "the promise of the father," symbolizing the giving of the Holy Spirit at Pentecost as an earnest deposit of the gift of eternal life.

Next, the father brings out the Matzah that was hidden. Each member is given two pieces of matzah to make the Afikomen. The Afikomen is a sandwich made of two pieces of matzah with the Maror (bitter herbs) on one side and the Charoset (a sweet antidote to the bitter herbs) on the other side. The sandwich is eaten Maror side first, then Charoset. This symbolizes that the Messiah is the only antidote for sin. Since it was forbidden to eat the Passover lamb anywhere except Jerusalem (Deuteronomy 16:5), together the group says:

"I am observing this commandment so I may remember the Passover lamb eaten at the end of the Seder. May the eating of the Afikomen achieve all the spiritual things accomplished by the Passover lamb itself."

During the first Passover at the Exodus, if one placed the blood of the Passover lamb on the door post, the death angel would not kill the firstborn in the house. Salvation was offered only if one believed in the protecting blood of the Passover lamb. Matzah is pierced and has stripes from being cooked unleavened. Isaiah makes allusion to this in Isaiah 53 when he says the Messiah was pierced for us and by His stripes we are healed.

At this point in the Seder ritual, Psalm 126 is sung and participants drink the third cup of wine. The first cup of wine is called the "cup of sanctification"; the second cup is the "cup of affliction"; the third cup is the "cup of redemption"; the fourth cup is the "cup of Elijah." Finally the fourth cup, the cup of Elijah, is poured. A child is then sent to the door to see if Elijah has returned that year. This shows the fact that Elijah and another witness will appear in the Temple in Jerusalem before the Second Coming of the Messiah. Then they sing the Hallel (which are Psalms 115-118 and Psalm 136).

O give thanks unto the LORD; for *He is* good: because His mercy *endureth* for ever. Let Israel now say, that His mercy *endureth* for ever. Let the house of Aaron now say, that His mercy *endureth* for ever. Let them now that fear the LORD say, that His mercy *endureth* for ever. I called upon the LORD in distress: the LORD answered me, *and set me* in a large place. The LORD *is* on my side; I will not fear: what can man do unto me? The LORD taketh my part with them that help me: therefore shall I see *my desire* upon them that hate me. *It is* better to trust in the LORD than to put confidence in man. *It is* better to trust in the LORD than to put confidence in princes. All nations compassed me about: but in the name of the LORD will I destroy them. They compassed me about; yea, they compassed me about: but in the name of the LORD I will destroy them. They compassed me about like bees; they are quenched as the fire of thorns: for in the name of the LORD I will destroy them. Thou hast thrust sore at me that I might fall: but the LORD helped me. The LORD *is* my strength and song, and is become my salvation. The voice of rejoicing and salvation *is* in the tabernacles of the righteous: the right hand of the LORD doeth valiantly. The right hand of the LORD is exalted: the right hand of the LORD doeth valiantly. I shall not die, but live, and declare the works of the LORD. The LORD hath chastened me sore: but He hath not given me over unto death. Open to me the gates of righteousness: I will go into them, *and* I will praise the LORD: This gate of the LORD, into which the righteous shall enter. I will praise Thee: for Thou hast heard me, and art become my salvation. The stone *which* the builders refused is become the head *stone* of the corner. This is the LORD'S doing; it *is* marvellous in our eyes. This *is* the day *which* the LORD hath made; we will rejoice and be glad in it. Save now, I beseech Thee, O LORD: O LORD, I beseech Thee, send now prosperity. Blessed *be* He that cometh in the name of the LORD: we have blessed You out of the house of the LORD. God *is* the LORD, which hath shewed us light: bind the sacrifice with cords, *even* unto the horns of the altar. Thou *art* my God, and I will praise Thee: *Thou art* my God, I

will exalt Thee. O give thanks unto the LORD; for *He is* good: for His mercy *endureth* for ever.
Psalms 118:1-29

Historical Notes

The lamb is killed on Nisan 14 at 3 PM. The lamb is cooked and all the other preparations are finished before 6 PM, when Nisan 15 begins. The Seder ritual was observed between 6 PM and 12 AM. The death angel passed by at 12 AM. Pharaoh summoned Moses to allow the children of Israel to go serve God on His Mountain. The children of Israel left Egypt in the Exodus between 12 AM and 6 AM on Nisan 15. This is why the Seder must begin at 6 PM and end before 12 AM.

When Joseph died, he was buried in the Egyptian city of Sukkot. But before his death, Joseph made his sons swear that when the prophecy was fulfilled, they would take his bones with them and bury him in Israel when they got there. So the first stop when they left Goshen was the Egyptian city of Sukkot, where Joseph was buried.

This is another typological prophecy. The festival of Sukkot teaches about the Messianic Kingdom. The rabbis call Egypt the seat of idolatry. A high place of child sacrifice to idols is called *Rama* in Hebrew. We can be assured that we are going to the Promised Land when we see that the tomb of Joseph of Rama (Arimathaea) is empty!

Matzah Bread

First John 3:5 records the Messiah was completely sinless. Leaven represents sin, and unleavened bread represents the Messiah being a sinless sacrifice for us. Jesus said "this is My body broken for you" referring to the matzeh or unleavened bread. He was buried on the first day of Unleavened Bread and remained in the grave until He resurrected on First Fruits. This festival of Unleavened Bread also teaches us to remain pure from sin. Paul explained it this way:

> Purge out therefore the old leaven, that ye may be a new lump, as ye are unleavened. For even Christ our passover is sacrificed for us: therefore let us keep the feast, not with old leaven, neither with the leaven of malice and wickedness; but with the unleavened *bread* of sincerity and truth. *1 Corinthians 5:7-8*

Matzah bread is pierced with holes to cook thoroughly because it has no leaven to make it rise. Because it is cooked upon an open grill, it also has stripes.

> And I will pour upon the house of David, and upon the inhabitants of Jerusalem, the spirit of grace and of supplications: and they shall look upon me whom they have pierced, and they shall mourn for him, as one mourneth for *his* only *son,* and shall be in bitterness for him, as one that is in bitterness for *his* firstborn. *Zechariah 12:10*

> For dogs have compassed me: the assembly of the wicked have inclosed me: they pierced my hands and my feet. *Psalms 22:16*

> But He *was* wounded for our transgressions, *He was* bruised for our iniquities: the chastisement of our peace *was* upon Him; and with His stripes we are healed. *Isaiah 53:5*

The Prophecy

The promise God gave to Abraham was fulfilled exactly 430 years later *to the day*, the very day of Passover / Unleavened Bread.

> And it came to pass at the end of the four hundred and thirty years, even the selfsame day it came to pass, that all the hosts of the LORD went out from the land of Egypt. *Exodus 12:41*

John 6:51 records that it was during a Passover in Galilee that Jesus taught that He was the bread of life.

John the Baptist's Birth

Zachariah was of the priestly course of Abijah. Each course served for one week twice a year. The week of the course of Abijah would be forty days after Passover in the month of Sivan, June/July, and again in Kislev, November/December.

> There was in the days of Herod, the king of Judaea, a certain priest named Zacharias, of the course of Abia: and his wife *was* of the daughters of Aaron, and her name *was* Elisabeth. *Luke 1:5*

> The seventh to Hakkoz, the eighth to Abijah, *1 Chronicles 24:10*

Since Zachariah was praying the traditional prayers for Pentecost, we know it was during the month of Sivan.

> And it came to pass, that, as soon as the days of his ministration were accomplished, he departed to his own house. And after those days his wife Elisabeth conceived... *Luke 1:23-24*

John the Baptist was conceived right after Zachariah's priestly duty was over. Based on the priestly purity laws we have to give or take up to two weeks, which places John's birth about the time of Passover.

Remember that part of the Seder ritual is to go to the door to see if Elijah has come that year. Perhaps this was a typological prophecy showing when John would be born.

For all the prophets and the law prophesied until John. And if ye will receive *it,* this is Elias, which was for to come. *Matthew 11:13-14*

Biblical events that occurred on Nisan 15
The Exodus occurred
John the Baptist born
Jesus began His three days and nights in the grave

First Fruits,
of the Barley Harvest

בכורים

Nissan						
S	M	T	W	T	F	S
					1	2
3	4	5	6	7	8	9
10	11	12	13	14	15	16
17	18	19	20	21	22	23
24	25	26	27	28	29	30

The festival of First Fruits (of the barley harvest) occurs on the first day of the week, or Sunday, after the high Sabbath of Unleavened Bread. The festival of Unleavened Bread always falls on Nisan 15.

> Speak unto the children of Israel, and say unto them, When ye be come into the land which I give unto you, and shall reap the harvest thereof, then ye shall bring a sheaf of the firstfruits of your harvest unto the priest: and he shall wave the sheaf before the LORD, to be accepted for you: on the morrow after the sabbath the priest shall wave it. *Leviticus 23:10-11*

Jesus was crucified on Passover, buried on Unleavened Bread, and resurrected on the first day of the week, at the end of the Sabbath, on First Fruits! We see this makes up the three days and nights Jesus was in the grave. The year Messiah died, First Fruits fell on Nissan 17. The apostle

Paul taught Jesus resurrected on the Festival of First Fruits.

But now is Christ risen from the dead, *and* become the firstfruits of them that slept. *1 Corinthians 15:20*

In the temple a ceremony is held on the Festival of First Fruits. Sheaves of barley are brought into the temple, ground into flour, then baked into cakes. This ritual shows the death of the grain and its resurrection into a new form. The apostle Paul wrote this First-Fruits ritual taught we will be resurrected in a glorified form which is different from the current corruptible bodies we are in now, just as Jesus was resurrected in a glorified body. Jesus was the first fruits to receive a glorified body that will never die. We, in like manner, will obtain those bodies in our resurrection.

For since by man *came* death, by man *came* also the resurrection of the dead. For as in Adam all die, even so in Christ shall all be made alive. But every man in his own order: Christ the firstfruits; afterward they that are Christ's at his coming. *1 Corinthians 15:21-23*

Thou fool, that which thou sowest is not quickened, except it die: and that which thou sowest, thou sowest not that body that shall be, but bare grain, it may chance of wheat, or of some other *grain...* So also *is* the resurrection of the dead. It is sown in corruption; it is raised in incorruption: it is sown in dishonour; it is raised in glory: it is sown in weakness; it is raised in power: it is sown a natural body; it is raised a spiritual body. There is a natural body, and there is a spiritual body. *1 Corinthians 15:36-37, 42-44*

Apostles' Teaching on First Fruits

Paul and Peter link the baptism of Moses in the Red Sea on the 17th of Nisan, and the ark landing after the Flood on the 17th of Nisan, with Jesus' resurrection on First Fruits on the 17th of Nisan.

For Christ also hath once suffered for sins, the just for the unjust, that He might bring us to God, being put to death in the flesh, but quickened by the Spirit: by which also He went and preached unto the spirits in prison; which sometime were disobedient, when once the longsuffering of God waited in the days of Noah, while the ark was a preparing, wherein few, that is, eight souls were saved by water. The like figure whereunto *even* baptism doth also now save us (not the putting away of the filth of the flesh, but the answer of a good conscience toward God,) by the resurrection of Jesus Christ: *1 Peter 3:18-21*

Moreover, brethren, I would not that ye should be ignorant, how that all our fathers were under the cloud, and all passed through the sea; and were all baptized unto Moses in the cloud and in the sea; and did all eat the same spiritual meat; and did all drink the same spiritual drink: for they drank of that spiritual Rock that followed them: and that Rock was Christ. *1 Corinthians 10:1-4*

The Talmud or Maimonides

The Talmud and Jasher (chapter 81) say the Israelites crossed the Red Sea on Nisan 21, not Nisan 17. However, Rambam calculated that the Israelites left Egypt on Nisan 15 and crossed the red Sea on Nissan 17 (See *The Biblical and Historical Background of the Jewish Holy Days* by Abraham Block, pg. 186).

Biblical events that occurred on Nisan 17
Noah's ark lands on dry ground
Children of Israel came up out of the Red Sea
Egyptian army died in the Red Sea (4th watch)
Ahasuerus executes Haman
Ahasuerus created a decree to help the Jews
Jesus Resurrected (4th watch)

Pentecost,
Weeks

שבועות

Nisan						
S	M	T	W	T	F	S
					1	2
3	4	5	6	7	8	9
10	11	12	13	14	15	16
17	18	19	20	21	22	23
24	25	26	27	28	29	30

Iyar						
S	M	T	W	T	F	S
1	2	3	4	5	6	7
8	9	10	11	12	13	14
15	16	17	18	19	20	21
22	23	24	25	26	27	28
29	30					

Sivan						
S	M	T	W	T	F	S
		1	2	3	4	5
6	7	8	9	10	11	12
13	14	15	16	17	18	19
20	21	22	23	24	25	26
27	28	29	30			

The festival of Pentecost commemorates the giving of the Law from Mount Sinai and the birth of the church as recorded in Acts 2. Other names for the festival of Pentecost are *Natan Torah* (giving of the Law), the festival of the "First Trump," and the festival of the *Kahalot*. The second tithe was given on Pentecost (Deut. 14:28).

> And ye shall count unto you from the morrow after the sabbath, from the day that ye brought the sheaf of the wave offering; seven sabbaths shall be complete: even unto the morrow after the seventh sabbath shall ye number fifty days; and ye shall offer a new meat offering unto the LORD... And ye shall proclaim on the selfsame day, *that* it may be an holy convocation unto you: ye shall do no servile work *therein: it shall be* a statute for ever in all your dwellings throughout your generations. *Leviticus 23:15-16,21*

From the "morrow after the [weekly] Sabbath," the 17th of Nisan, Jews start what is called the "counting of the omer." Each day is counted until we reach the fiftieth day, Sivan 6. Sivan 6 would be from Saturday night to Sunday night. This marks the day when Moses came down from Mount Sinai and delivered the Ten Commandments to the children of Israel. This is also the day when the disciples were gathered for the Pentecost service Sunday morning and at 9 AM the Holy Spirit fell.

> And when the day of Pentecost was fully come, they were all with one accord in one place. And suddenly there came a sound from heaven as of a rushing mighty wind, and it filled all the house where they were sitting. And there appeared unto them cloven tongues like as of fire, and it sat upon each of them. And they were all filled with the Holy Ghost, and

began to speak with other tongues, as the Spirit gave them utterance. *Acts 2:1-4*

Tongues of Fire - The Giving of the Law

Moses received the Ten Commandments written directly with the finger of God from within fire.

And the LORD delivered unto me two tables of stone written with the finger of God; and on them *was written* according to all the words, which the LORD spake with you in the mount out of the midst of the fire in the day of the assembly. *Deuteronomy 9:10*

God spoke from the clouds and the fire. The italicized words are word or phrases added by the translators to clarify the passage. Sometimes it confuses the passages. In Deuteronomy 4, Moses said when God spoke the people did not see Him, they only saw "the voice." This "voice" was in the form of fire.

And ye came near and stood under the mountain; and the mountain burned with fire unto the midst of heaven, with darkness, clouds, and thick darkness. And the LORD spake unto you out of the midst of the fire: ye heard the voice of the words, but saw no similitude; only *ye heard* a voice. *Deuteronomy 4:11-12*

In Hebrews, the phrase "voice of words" from Deuteronomy is translated into Greek with the word for "voice" being singular and the word for "words" being plural. The Greek word for "words" is *Rhema*. Rhema, as opposed to Logos, means a specific word of knowledge or wisdom from one person.

For ye are not come unto the mount that might be touched, and that burned with fire, nor unto blackness, and darkness, and tempest, and the sound of a trumpet, and the voice of words; which *voice* they that heard entreated that the word should not be spoken to them any more: *Hebrews 12:18-19*

So is Scripture telling us that God spoke in seventy languages on that day of Pentecost when the Law was given and that it was visibly seen as tongues of fire? That is what the ancient rabbis taught.

On the occasion of the giving of the Torah, the children of Israel not only heard the Lord's voice but actually saw the sound waves as they emerged from the Lord's mouth. They visualized them as a fiery substance. Each commandment that left the Lord's mouth traveled around the entire camp and then finally the fiery substance which they saw engraved itself on the tablets. *Mirash says on Shmot pg. 182*

"When God gave the Law on Mt. Sinai, He displayed untold marvels to Israel with His voice. What happened? God spoke and the voice reverberated throughout the whole land... it says, the people witnessed the thunderings (Exodus 18:15). Note that it does not say "the thunder," but "the thunderings;" wherefore Rabbi Johanan said that God's voice, as it was uttered, split into seventy languages, so that all the nations should understand." *Exodus Rabbah 5:9*

"The Revelation at Sinai, it was taught, was given in desert territory, which belongs to one nation exclusively; and it was not heard by Israel alone, but by the inhabitants of all the earth. The Divine Voice divided itself into the seventy tongues then spoken on the earth, so that all the children of men might understand its world-embracing and man-redeeming message." *Rabbi Joseph Hertz, Authorized Daily Prayer Book, pg. 791*

Tongues of Fire - Birth of the Church

What is interesting about these legends is that about 1,500 years later, on another Pentecost, as the Holy Spirit was given at the birth of the church, cloven tongues of fire could be seen resting on the heads of believers. This time the believers were filled with the Holy Spirit and each believer spoke in a foreign language. Acts 2 lists seventeen different foreign languages, but I believe it was a lot more.

"And how hear we every man in our own tongue, wherein we were born? Parthians, and Medes, and Elamites, and the dwellers in Mesopotamia, and in Judaea, and Cappadocia, in Pontus, and Asia, Phrygia, and Pamphylia, in Egypt, and in the parts of Libya about Cyrene, and strangers of Rome, Jews and proselytes, Cretes and Arabians, we do hear them speak in our tongues the wonderful works of God." *Acts 2:8-11*

Peter recorded that all these things were a partial fulfillment of the prophecy given by Joel:

"But this is that which was spoken by the prophet Joel; And it shall come to pass in the last days, saith God, I will pour out of my Spirit upon all flesh: and your sons and your daughters shall prophesy, and your young men shall see visions, and your old men shall dream dreams: and on my servants and on my handmaidens I will pour out in those days of my Spirit; and they shall prophesy: and I will shew

wonders in heaven above, and signs in the earth beneath; blood, and fire, and vapour of smoke: the sun shall be turned into darkness, and the moon into blood, before the great and notable day of the Lord come: and it shall come to pass, that whosoever shall call on the name of the Lord shall be saved."
Acts 2:16-21

The First Trump

Genesis 22 records the story of God testing Abraham by ordering him to go to Mt. Moriah and sacrifice his son Isaac. At the last moment, the Angel of the Lord stopped Abraham from killing his son and provided a ram as a substitute sacrifice. Genesis 22:3-4 showed after God spoke to Abraham, he rose early the next day and traveled for three days to Mount Moriah. The Jewish Midrash states Isaac was born on Nisan 15 and that when Abraham started to sacrifice Isaac, it was on his thirty-third or thirty-seventh birthday. This is a picture of Jesus' death on the cross. Abraham left on Nisan 10 and started the sacrifice on Nisan 14. So it was the same place and day of the Messiah's sacrifice.

God provided a ram that was caught in a thicket by its two horns. Ram horns are called shofars and are used as musical instruments. The ancient rabbis taught that the ram was a picture of the salvation the Messiah would bring to all mankind. They also taught that as the ram's horns are an outgrowth of the ram itself, the ram's two horns represented an outgrowth of the Messiah's salvation. Its left horn was connected with the law God gave on Mt. Sinai, which is why the festival of Pentecost is also called the festival of the First Trump.

We will see in the chapter about trumpets that for the same reason, the right horn is connected to the resurrection of the dead, which is why the festival of trumpets is also called the festival of the Last Trump.

The ancient rabbis said the left horn represented the birth of Israel and the right horn represented Israel's complete restoration when the Messiah comes. In other words, the horns represent the giving of the Law on Mt. Sinai and the resurrection of the dead. The rabbis also connected them with the Jewish wedding ceremony. See the chapter on the wedding ceremony for full details. Christians recognize this as true; but also see the festivals of the first and last trumps as teaching about the birth of the church and the Rapture.

The Church - Kahalot

Another name for the festival of Pentecost was the festival of *Kahalot*. This Hebrew word means an assembly. The matching New Testament Greek word is Ecclesia, which literally means "called out ones." It is the Greek word used for "church" in the New Testament.

This teaches us that Pentecost would be the birth of the end-time church, the assembly full of the Holy Spirit, as prophesied in Jeremiah 31, Zechariah 3, and other places.

Notice the difference. On the first Pentecost when Moses brought the Ten Commandments down from Mount Sinai 3,000 rebellious Jews were destroyed. On the Second Pentecost when the church was born, 3,000 Jews were saved!

Biblical events that occurred on Pentecost
Law given on Mt. Sinai
Birth of the Church

Latter Rain (fall) Festivals

5. Trumpets
    The Return
    Days of Awe

6. Atonement

7. Tabernacles
    The Great Day
    The Eighth Conclusion
    The Rejoicings in the Torah

The Return, Teshuvah

תשוה

Elul						
S	M	T	W	T	F	S
			1	2	3	4
5	6	7	8	9	10	11
12	13	14	15	16	17	18
19	20	21	22	23	24	25
26	27	28	29	30		

Tishrei						
S	M	T	W	T	F	S
					1	2
3	4	5	6	7	8	9
10	11	12	13	14	15	16
17	18	19	20	21	22	23
24	25	26	27	28	29	30

The season of *Teshuvah* is a forty-day period starting on Elul 1 and ending on Tishrei 10. It consists of thirty days of preparation for the first ten days of Tishrei, referred to as the High Holy Days. Teshuvah is a Hebrew word that means "repentance" and "return." During the first thirty days, we should be in an attitude of repentance awaiting the return of the Messiah.

Scripture Reading

Each morning of the forty days of Teshuvah, after the normal morning prayers, a shofar is blown and Psalm 27 is read. Psalm 27 is a warning that the time of Jacob's trouble (Jeremiah 30:7) is approaching. However, those who look to God will have nothing to fear.

Psalm 27 A Psalm of **David.** The LORD *is* my light and my salvation; whom shall I fear? The LORD *is* the strength of my life; of whom shall I be afraid? When the wicked, *even* mine enemies and my foes, came upon me to eat up my flesh, they stumbled and fell. Though an host should encamp against me, my heart shall not fear: though war should rise against me, in this *will* I *be* confident. One *thing* have I desired of the LORD, that will I seek after; that I may dwell in the house of the LORD all the days of my life, to behold the beauty of the LORD, and to enquire in His temple. For in the time of trouble He shall hide me in His pavilion: in the secret of His tabernacle shall He hide me; He shall set me up upon a rock. And now shall mine head be lifted up above mine enemies round about me: therefore will I offer in His tabernacle sacrifices of joy; I will sing, yea, I will sing praises unto the LORD. Hear, O LORD, *when* I cry with my voice: have mercy also upon me, and answer me. *When Thou saidst,* Seek ye My face; my heart said unto Thee, Thy face, LORD, will I seek. Hide not Thy face *far* from me; put not Thy servant away in anger: Thou hast been my help; leave me not, neither forsake me, O God of my salvation. When my father and my mother forsake me, then the LORD will take me up. Teach me Thy way, O LORD, and lead me in a plain path, because of mine enemies. Deliver me not over unto the will of mine enemies: for false witnesses are risen up against me, and such as breathe out cruelty. *I had fainted,* unless I had believed to see the goodness of the LORD in the land of the living. Wait on the LORD: be of good courage, and He shall strengthen thine heart: wait, I say, on the LORD. *Psalms 27:1-14*

After this, Ezekiel 33:1-7 is read.

Ezekiel 33 Again the word of the LORD came unto me, saying, son of man, speak to the children of thy people, and say unto them, When I bring the sword upon a land, if the people of the land take a man of their coasts, and set him for their watchman: if when he seeth the sword come upon the land, he blow the trumpet, and warn the people; then whosoever heareth the sound of the trumpet, and taketh not warning; if the sword come, and take him away, his blood shall be upon his own head. He heard the sound of the trumpet, and took not warning; his blood shall be upon him. But he that taketh warning shall deliver his soul. But if the watchman see the sword come, and blow not the trumpet, and the people be not warned; if the sword come, and take *any* person from among them, he is taken away in his iniquity; but his blood will I require at the watchman's hand. So thou, O son of man, I have set thee a watchman unto the house of Israel; therefore thou shalt hear the word at my mouth, and warn them from me. *Ezekiel 33:1-7*

In some places Zephaniah 1:14-2:3 is also read.

The great day of the LORD *is* near, *it is* near, and hasteth greatly, *even* the voice of the day of the LORD: the mighty man shall cry there bitterly. That day *is* a day of wrath, a day of trouble and distress, a day of wasteness and desolation, a day of darkness

and gloominess, a day of clouds and thick darkness, a day of the trumpet and alarm against the fenced cities, and against the high towers. And I will bring distress upon men, that they shall walk like blind men, because they have sinned against the LORD: and their blood shall be poured out as dust, and their flesh as the dung. Neither their silver nor their gold shall be able to deliver them in the day of the LORD'S wrath; but the whole land shall be devoured by the fire of His jealousy: for He shall make even a speedy riddance of all them that dwell in the land. Gather yourselves together, yea, gather together, O nation not desired; before the decree bring forth, *before* the day pass as the chaff, before the fierce anger of the LORD come upon you, before the day of the LORD'S anger come upon you. Seek ye the LORD, all ye meek of the earth, which have wrought His judgment; seek righteousness, seek meekness: it may be ye shall be hid in the day of the LORD'S anger.
Zephaniah 1:14-2:1-3

In some messianic synagogues, Hosea 6 is also read. In verse one the word "return" is Teshuvah. This passage is interpreted as after two days, after the Roman dispersion, the millennial reign will begin, which is typified by the Latter Rain festival of Teshuvah.

Come, and let us return unto the LORD: for He hath torn, and He will heal us; He hath smitten, and He will bind us up. After two days will He revive us: in the third day He will raise us up, and we shall live in His sight. Then shall we know, *if* we follow on to know the LORD: His going forth is prepared as the morning; and He shall come unto us as the rain, as the latter *and* former rain unto the earth. *Hosea 6:1-3*

The Romans destroyed the Temple in AD 70 and the great dispersion occurred at the end of the Bar-Kokhba rebellion in AD 132. After 1,816 years the Jews returned to their land in AD 1948. See *Ancient Prophecies Revealed* for more details on the many prophecies fulfilled since the dispersion and the fifty-three fulfilled since AD 1948.

During Teshuvah, usually on the day prior to Rosh Hashanah, the shofar is blown. This time it is blown with about one hundred very short blasts, followed by one very long blast. Then the congregation says "the gates of heaven are now open." This represents the blowing of the trump that raises the dead and raptures the believers. This occurs only when the gates of heaven are open.

The ancient rabbis said when you see the festival language "the opening of the gates" in Scripture, it may be referring to the time of the Resurrection.

Trumpets,
Rosh Hashanah

ראש השנה

Tishrei						
S	M	T	W	T	F	S
					1	2
3	4	5	6	7	8	9
10	11	12	13	14	15	16
17	18	19	20	21	22	23
24	25	26	27	28	29	30

Speak unto the children of Israel, saying, In the seventh month, in the first *day* of the month, shall ye have a sabbath, a memorial of blowing of trumpets, an holy convocation. *Leviticus 23:24*

This festival is known by many names because it represents many things. It is called the Festival of Trumpets based on the above passage. It is also called Rosh Hashanah, meaning the "head of the year" or New Year's Day. It occurs on Tishrei 1. See the Encyclopedia Judaica for more information on its various names.

New Year's Day - Rosh Hashanah
The rabbis taught that New Year's Day was exactly that, the day of creation. Adam was created on the sixth day, which is Tishrei 6. Challah bread is served at all the festivals. On Rosh Hashanah, a special round challah bread is made to symbolize the world. Some place a

candle on this challah bread to celebrate the birthday of the world.

Rosh Hashanah has no specific ritual to be performed on a special hour (like Passover does: 3 PM on Nisan 14). It is a two-day festival, so no man knows the hour or the day when the events it predicts will actually occur.

Day of the Awakening Blast - Yom Turah

Another name is the Festival of the Awakening Blast. This name is based on the following passage in Numbers:

> And in the seventh month, on the first *day* of the month, ye shall have an holy convocation; ye shall do no servile work: it is a day of blowing the trumpets unto you. *Numbers 29:1*

The Hebrew for the words "day of blowing of trumpets" is literally *Yom Turah*, the day of the awakening blast. Turah is an awakening blast from the shofar that would be the signal for an army to wake up and prepare for the day's battle. Turah is also translated "shout." The rabbis took this to mean this is the day of the resurrection of the dead.

> Open ye the gates, that the righteous nation which keepeth the truth may enter in... LORD, in trouble have they visited Thee, they poured out a prayer *when* Thy chastening *was* upon them. Like as a woman with child, *that* draweth near the time of her delivery, is in pain, *and* crieth out in her pangs; so have we been in Thy sight, O LORD. We have been with child, we have been in pain, we have as it were brought forth wind; we have not wrought any deliverance in the earth; neither have the inhabitants of the world fallen. Thy dead *men* shall live, *together*

with my dead body shall they arise. Awake and sing, ye that dwell in dust: for thy dew *is as* the dew of herbs, and the earth shall cast out the dead. Come, my people, enter thou into thy chambers, and shut thy doors about thee: hide thyself as it were for a little moment, until the indignation be overpast. For, behold, the LORD cometh out of his place to punish the inhabitants of the earth for their iniquity: the earth also shall disclose her blood, and shall no more cover her slain. *Isaiah 26:2,16-21*

Isaiah mentions the "gates are open" which refers to Rosh Hashanah. Notice the resurrection of the dead occurs at the same time the righteous nation enters into the bridal chamber (Chedar) and is hidden until the indignation is past (until the seven-year Tribulation is over).

"The resurrection of the dead will occur on Yom haDin, which is also called Rosh Hashanah," *Talmud, Rosh Hashanah 16b*

"It has been taught: Rabbi Eliezer says, 'In the month of Tishri the world was created, ...and in Tishrei they will be redeemed in the time to come.'" *Talmud, Rosh Hashanah 10b-11a*

The Opening of the Gates

At the end of the *musaf* sacrifices, the trumpet would blow the loudest and the people would shout "the gates of heaven are open!" This teaches about the Resurrection and Rapture. Many passages refer to a door or gates being opened and the Resurrection occurring; the righteous enter into the wedding chamber until the wrath is over; and the Lamb of God is crowned King. Here are just a few.

In that day shall this song be sung in the land of Judah; we have a strong city; salvation will *God* appoint *for* walls and bulwarks. Open ye the **gates**, that the righteous nation which keepeth the truth may enter in. Thou wilt keep *him* in perfect peace, *whose* mind *is* stayed *on Thee:* because he trusteth in Thee... Thy dead *men* shall live, *together with* my dead body shall they arise. Awake and sing, ye that dwell in dust: for thy dew *is as* the dew of herbs, and the earth shall cast out the dead. Come, my people, enter thou into thy chambers, and shut thy doors about thee: hide thyself as it were for a little moment, until the indignation be overpast. For, behold, the LORD cometh out of His place to punish the inhabitants of the earth for their iniquity: the earth also shall disclose her blood, and shall no more cover her slain. *Isaiah 26:1-3, 19-21*

The righteous perisheth, and no man layeth *it* to heart: and merciful men *are* taken away, none considering that the righteous is taken away from the evil *to come.* He shall enter into peace: they shall rest in their beds, *each one* walking *in* His uprightness. *Isaiah 57:1-2*

Lift ye up a banner upon the high mountain, exalt the voice unto them, shake the hand, that they may go into the **gates** of the nobles. *Isaiah 13:2*

After this I looked, and, behold, a **door** *was* opened in heaven: and the first voice which I heard *was* as it were of a trumpet talking with me; which said, Come up hither, and I will shew thee things which must be hereafter. *Revelation 4:1*

Day of Concealment - Yom HaKeseh

Every Jewish calendar month starts on a new moon. See the chapter on the New Moon Festival for details. Rosh Hashanah will always be on a new moon since it is the first and second of Tishrei. But this is a special new moon called *Yom HaKeseh*. Yom HaKeseh means "the Day of Concealment." The term was taken from Psalm 81:3 by the ancient rabbis.

"Blow up the trumpet in the new moon, in the time appointed, on our solemn feast day." *Psalm 81:3*

The Hebrew word "Keseh" is translated "time appointed" in this passage, but actually means to conceal. A new moon is said to be concealed as opposed to a full moon. This is yet another picture of the concealment of the church by the Rapture.

The Last Trump

Another name for Rosh Hashanah is the Festival of the Last Trump. Rabbi Herman Kieval wrote *The High Holy Days,* which was first published in 1959. In his work he states that many Jewish scholars, including Theodore Gaster, have taught that the festival of Rosh Hashanah was called the Festival of the Last Trump from ancient times.

In an ancient Jewish midrash called *Prike deR' Eliezer,* the origin of these terms is explained. The left horn of the ram sacrificed by Abraham in place of Isaac, is called the first trump, and was blown on Mount Sinai. Its right horn, called the last trump, will be blown to herald the coming of the Messiah. See the chapter on Pentecost for details.

The ancient rabbis said the left horn represented the birth of Israel and the right horn represented Israel's complete restoration when the Messiah comes. In other words, the horns represent the giving of the Law on Mt. Sinai and the resurrection of the dead. The horns were also connected with the Jewish wedding ceremony. See the chapter on the wedding ceremony for full details. Christians recognize this as true, but also see the festivals of the first and last trumps as teaching about the birth of the church and the Rapture.

The apostle Paul taught the Rapture would occur at the "last trump" and with the "shout" or "turah" of the Archangel.

> "Behold, I shew you a mystery; we shall not all sleep, but we shall all be changed, in a moment, in the twinkling of an eye, at the last trump: for the trumpet shall sound, and the dead shall be raised incorruptible, and we shall be changed." *I Corinthians 15:51-52*

> For the Lord himself shall descend from heaven with a shout, with the voice of the archangel, and with the trump of God: and the dead in Christ shall rise first: then we which are alive *and* remain shall be caught up together with them in the clouds, to meet the Lord in the air: and so shall we ever be with the Lord.
> *1 Thessalonians 4:16-17*

Natzal

Part of the ritual for Rosh Hashanah consists of the *zikhronot*, or Book of Remembrance being opened and the *Natzal* occurring. Natzal is the Hebrew word that corresponds to the Greek word *harpizo*. Harpizo is the New Testament Greek word we translate as Rapture. Natzal means "a catching away."

Although the word natzal is not found directly in Scripture, the rabbis coined the term based on passages like Zephaniah 2:1-3 (See the chapter on Teshuvah) where the whole righteous nation is hidden before the day of the Lord's anger, which consisted of both the living and the dead in Messiah; and Daniel 12:2-3 where the dead are raised, then the wise [living believers] shine [obtain glorified bodies].

So the Scriptural word "gathering" is used of the hiding of both the living and dead believers. But the word natzal refers to the living believers who are changed, then hidden with the rest. The rabbis compared this to both Enoch and Elijah being changed, then caught up.

Why the "last trump" cannot be the seventh trump.
Many Christians who are ignorant of the seven festivals *assume* that when Paul wrote of the "last trump" in 1 Corinthians 15:52-53 he was referring to the seventh trumpet in Revelation 11:15. One major problem with this point of view is that Paul wrote 1 Corinthians before his death in AD 67. John wrote the book of Revelation in AD 95. Paul could not be quoting a book written more than twenty-five years after his death! Knowing these things, let us go on and see what we can learn about the seven-year Tribulation period from these festivals.

Silver Trumpets
In Numbers 10, God commanded Moses to create two silver trumpets. They were blown for various reasons, but only one would be blown to call the nobles to the Temple.

Make thee two trumpets of silver; of a whole piece shalt thou make them: that thou mayest use them for the calling of the assembly, and for the journeying of the camps. And when they shall blow with them, all the assembly shall assemble themselves to thee at the door of the tabernacle of the congregation. And if they blow *but* with one *trumpet,* then the princes, *which are* heads of the thousands of Israel, shall gather themselves unto thee. *Numbers 10:2-4*

In one of the temple rituals, three priests ascend to the trumpeting stone on one of the corners of the temple and blow the two silver trumpets and one shofar. This was always done to signal the beginning of the Sabbath or festivals. First the priest on the left would blow a silver trumpet; then the priest on the right would blow the second silver trumpet. Finally, the priest in the middle would sound the shofar.

On Rosh Hashanah this order would change. The priest on the left would sound the shofar, then the priest on the right would sound another shofar. Finally the priest in the middle would blow the silver trumpet. Moses wrote in Numbers 10 that if only *one* silver trump is blown, it is a signal for the nobles to ascend. And Peter and John tell us we are a race of kings and priests (nobles).

But ye *are* a chosen generation, a royal priesthood, an holy nation, a peculiar people; that ye should shew forth the praises of him who hath called you out of darkness into his marvellous light: *1 Peter 2:9*

And hath made us kings and priests unto God and his Father; to him *be* glory and dominion for ever and ever. Amen. *Revelation 1:6*

Day of the King - HaMelek

Rosh Hashanah is also called *Yom HaMelek,* or the Day of the King. It is the time of Messiah's coronation and the beginning of His kingdom. Compare this to passages like Daniel 7:13-14 and Revelation 5:1-14.

If a new king was to be crowned that year, the coronation would occur on the festival of Rosh Hashanah. When this happened, Psalm 45 wais read. Notice the first phrase of this Psalm tells us it is to be sung according to the tune of Shoshannim which is usually translated as "the Lillies." The Artscroll commentary on Tehillim (Psalms) states that the correct rendering is "set to the trumpet." A King always has his bride with him at his coronation.

Psalm 45: To the chief Musician upon Shoshannim, for the sons of Korah, Maschil, A Song of love.
My heart is inditing a good matter: I speak of the things which I have made touching the king: my tongue *is* the pen of a ready writer. Thou art fairer than the children of men: grace is poured into thy lips: therefore God hath blessed thee for ever. Gird thy sword upon *thy* thigh, O *most* mighty, with thy glory and thy majesty. And in thy majesty ride prosperously because of truth and meekness *and* righteousness; and thy right hand shall teach thee terrible things. Thine arrows *are* sharp in the heart of the king's enemies; *whereby* the people fall under thee. Thy throne, O God, *is* for ever and ever: the sceptre of thy kingdom *is* a right sceptre. Thou lovest righteousness, and hatest wickedness: therefore God, thy God, hath anointed thee with the oil of gladness above thy fellows. All thy garments *smell* of myrrh, and aloes, *and* cassia, out of the ivory palaces, whereby they have made thee glad. Kings' daughters *were* among thy honourable women: upon thy right hand did stand the queen in gold of Ophir. Hearken, O daughter, and consider, and incline thine ear; forget also thine own

people, and thy father's house; so shall the king greatly desire thy beauty: for He *is* thy Lord; and worship thou Him. And the daughter of Tyre *shall be there* with a gift; *even* the rich among the people shall entreat thy favour. The king's daughter *is* all glorious within: her clothing *is* of wrought gold. She shall be brought unto the king in raiment of needlework: the virgins her companions that follow her shall be brought unto thee. With gladness and rejoicing shall they be brought: they shall enter into the king's palace. Instead of thy fathers shall be thy children, whom thou mayest make princes in all the earth. I will make thy name to be remembered in all generations: therefore shall the people praise thee for ever and ever. *Psalms 45:1-17*

Psalm 47 is read *seven times* on Rosh Hashanah:

To the chief Musician, A Psalm for the sons of Korah. O clap your hands, all ye people; shout unto God with the voice of triumph. For the LORD most high *is* terrible; *He is* a great King over all the earth. He shall subdue the people under us, and the nations under our feet. He shall choose our inheritance for us, the excellency of Jacob whom He loved. Selah. God is gone up with a shout, the LORD with the sound of a trumpet. Sing praises to God, sing praises: sing praises unto our King, sing praises. For God *is* the King of all the earth: sing ye praises with understanding. God reigneth over the heathen: God sitteth upon the throne of his holiness. The princes of the people are gathered together, *even* the people of the God of Abraham: for the shields of the earth *belong* unto God: He is greatly exalted. *Psalms 47:1-9*

Psalms 48 and 2 are read, then finally part of Psalm 24.

Psalm 48: A Song *and* Psalm for the sons of Korah. Great *is* the LORD, and greatly to be praised in the city of our God, *in* the mountain of his holiness. Beautiful for situation, the joy of the whole earth, *is* mount Zion, *on* the sides of the north, the city of the great King. God is known in her palaces for a refuge. For, lo, the kings were assembled, they passed by together. They saw *it, and* so they marvelled; they were troubled, *and* hasted away. Fear took hold upon them there, *and* pain, as of a woman in travail. Thou breakest the ships of Tarshish with an east wind. As we have heard, so have we seen in the city of the LORD of hosts, in the city of our God: God will establish it for ever. Selah. We have thought of Thy lovingkindness, O God, in the midst of Thy temple. According to Thy name, O God, so *is* Thy praise unto the ends of the earth: Thy right hand is full of righteousness. Let mount Zion rejoice, let the daughters of Judah be glad, because of Thy judgments. Walk about Zion, and go round about her: tell the towers thereof. Mark ye well her bulwarks, consider her palaces; that ye may tell *it* to the generation following. For this God *is* our God for ever and ever: He will be our guide *even* unto death. *Psalms 48:1-14*

Psalm 2 Why do the heathen rage, and the people imagine a vain thing? The kings of the earth set themselves, and the rulers take counsel together, against the LORD, and against his Anointed [Messiah], *saying,* Let us break their bands asunder, and cast away their cords from us. He that sitteth in the heavens shall laugh: the Lord shall have them in derision. Then shall He speak unto them in His wrath, and vex them in His sore displeasure. Yet have I set My king upon My holy hill of Zion. I will declare the decree: the LORD hath said unto Me, Thou *art* my Son; this day have I begotten Thee. Ask of Me, and I shall give *Thee* the heathen *for* Thine inheritance, and the uttermost parts of the earth *for* Thy possession. Thou shalt break them with a rod of iron; Thou shalt dash them in pieces like a potter's vessel. Be wise now therefore, O ye kings: be instructed, ye judges of the earth. Serve the LORD with fear, and rejoice with trembling. Kiss the Son, lest He be angry, and ye perish *from* the way, when His wrath is kindled but a little. Blessed *are* all they that put their trust in Him. *Psalms 2:1-12*

Lift up your heads, O ye gates; and be ye lift up, ye everlasting doors; and the King of glory shall come in. Who *is* this King of glory? The LORD strong and mighty, the LORD mighty in battle. Lift up your heads, O ye gates; even lift *them* up, ye everlasting doors; and the King of glory shall come in. Who is this King of glory? The LORD of hosts, He *is* the King of glory. Selah. *Psalms 24:7-10*

Day of Remembrance - Yom Hazikkaron

Another title for Rosh Hashanah is *Yom HaZikkaron*, which means the Day of Remembrance. The rabbis took this name from Leviticus 23:24. It is a memorial day. The word for memorial in this passage is *zikkaron* or remembrance.

Speak unto the children of Israel, saying, In the seventh month, in the first *day* of the month, shall ye have a sabbath, a memorial of blowing of trumpets, an holy convocation. *Leviticus 23:24*

From Malachi the rabbis taught this is also when the Book of Remembrance is opened and the righteous are judged according to their works (Bema Judgment seat described in 2 Corinthians 5) after which God will judge the wicked (Sheep and Goat Judgment described in Matthew 25).[c]

> Then they that feared the LORD spake often one to another: and the LORD hearkened, and heard *it,* and a book of remembrance was written before him for them that feared the LORD, and that thought upon his name. And they shall be mine, saith the LORD of hosts, in that day when I make up my jewels; and I will spare them, as a man spareth his own son that serveth him. Then shall ye return, and discern between the righteous and the wicked, between him that serveth God and him that serveth him not.
> *Malachi 3:16-18*

The Day of Remembrance, Yom HaZikkaron, concerns a judgment of how much a believer will be rewarded; but the Day of Judgment, Yom HaDin, reveals a judgment regarding how much an unbeliever will be punished.

A Day of Remembrance also refers to the time when people bring gifts to the bride during the seven-day honeymoon.

The Day of Judgment - Yom HaDin
Another title for the festival of Trumpets is *Yom HaDin,* the Day of Judgment. This is the time when God sits on His throne and judges mankind. This is seen in many

---

[c] The Bema Judgment seat is when rewards are given to Christians after the Rapture and before the Second Coming. The Judgment of the sheep and goats is the judgment of nations immediately after the Second Coming.

passages like Daniel 7:9-10. Ezekiel 20:33-44 shows God as the Shepherd judging His sheep by passing them under the rod. Matthew 25:31-46 also illustrates the Day of Judgment as the Sheep and Goat Judgment. The ancient rabbis stated anytime we see God sitting in judgment in Scripture it must Judgment day or Rosh Hashanah.

Rabbinical tradition says that the people will be judged on a Rosh Hashanah. The books are opened and each person's name appears in one of three books. The Book of Life contains the names of the Righteous, those who trusted in God and the Messiah for deliverance and are granted eternal life. The Book of Death contains the names of the wicked, those who have rejected the Messiah and are damned. The third book, the Book of the Sinners, contains the names of those who have not yet made any decisions for or against the Messiah. Everyone is born with their name written in the Book of Sinners. If one accepts the Messiah and his free gift of eternal life, his name is blotted out of the Book of Sinners and written in the Book of Life. If one has not trusted in Messiah by the time he dies, his name is blotted out of the Book of Sinners and written into the Book of Death.

Other Events to take place on Rosh Hashanah

Ezra read the Scriptures and rededicated the people and the Temple Mount on Rosh Hashanah. Ezra offered sacrifices before they started laying the foundation of the temple (Nehemiah 7 and 8; Ezra 3:6). This will probably be the pattern when the next temple construction begins: sacrifices first, then the laying of the foundation stone.

Biblical events that occur on Rosh Hashanah

Creation
Ezra's rededication of the people
Sacrifices begin before Temple construction

Days of Awe,
Yamin Noraim

ימין נוראים

Tishrei						
S	M	T	W	T	F	S
					1	2
3	4	5	6	7	8	9
10	11	12	13	14	15	16
17	18	19	20	21	22	23
24	25	26	27	28	29	30

Those who did not heed Ezekiel's warning (given every day during Tesuvah) must enter the Days of Awe.

The time between Rosh Hashanah and Yom Kippur are called the *Yomin Noraim*, which means the "Days of Awe" or the terrible days. The ancient rabbis took this name from Joel 2:11, which refers to the Day of the Lord.

> "The LORD utters His voice before His army; surely His camp is very great, for strong is he who carries out His word. The day of the LORD is indeed great and very awesome [Nora], and who can endure it?" *Joel 2:11*

The Talmud also refers to this as the time of Jacob's Trouble. The ancient rabbis took this term from the prophet Jeremiah.

Ask ye now, and see whether a man doth travail with child? Wherefore do I see every man with his hands on his loins, as a woman in travail, and all faces are turned into paleness? Alas! for that day *is* great, so that none *is* like it: it *is* even the time of Jacob's trouble; but he shall be saved out of it.
Jeremiah 30:6-7

Notice, the Yomin Noraim are the seven days/years that occur between the Rapture/Resurrection of Rosh Hashanah and the Second Coming of Yom Kippur! This gives a perfect picture of the time of Jacob's trouble or the seven-year Tribulation period.

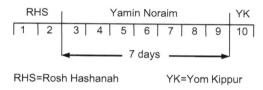

RHS=Rosh Hashanah   YK=Yom Kippur

Rosh Hashanah - Two Days
The festival of Rosh Hashanah is a two day festival occurring on the first and second of Tishrei.

"From the time of R. Johanan b. Zakkai; Palestine, like other countries, observed Rosh Hashanah for two days. The Zohar lays stress on the universal observance of two days."
Jewishencyclopedia.com; New-Year

This is also seen in Scripture. Ezra conducted services on the first and second of Tishrei and stated they were holy.

And Ezra the priest brought the law before the congregation both of men and women, and all that could hear with understanding, upon the first day of the seventh month... So the Levites stilled all the people, saying, Hold your peace, for the day *is* holy... And on the second day were gathered together the chief of the fathers of all the people, the priests, and the Levites, unto Ezra the scribe, even to understand the words of the law. *Nehemiah 8:2,11,13*

From this passage the ancient rabbis taught that Rosh Hashanah was to be thought of as one long 48-hour day. We will see that the festival of the Eighth Conclusion is another long 48-hour day.

Drawing by Clarence Larkin, 1907

Leviathan

We see the seven-headed red dragon in the book of Revelation. All the ancient cultures in the Middle East including Israel, Babylon, and the Arab peoples had a concept of a seven-headed sea creature they all called Leviathan, which represented an evil empire that would appear at the end of time.

From Job 41 the ancient rabbis believed that Leviathan was a terrible beast that was king of the children of pride, and that he would make a covenant with many and break that covenant (not be a servant forever). See the chapter on the Festival of Atonement for details on Leviathan's banquet / feast.

Job 41 Canst thou draw out leviathan with an hook? or his tongue with a cord *which* thou lettest down? Canst thou put an hook into his nose? or bore his jaw through with a thorn? Will he make many supplications unto thee? Will he speak soft *words* unto thee? Will he make a **covenant** with thee? Wilt thou take him for a **servant** for ever? Wilt thou play with him as *with* a bird? Or wilt thou bind him for thy maidens? Shall the companions make **a banquet** of him? Shall they part him among the merchants? Canst thou fill his skin with barbed irons? or his head with fish spears? Lay thine hand upon him, remember the battle, do no more. Behold, the hope of him is in vain: shall not *one* be cast down even at the sight of him? None *is so* fierce that dare stir him up: who then is able to stand before me? Who hath prevented me, that I should repay *him? Whatsoever is* under the whole heaven is mine. I will not conceal his parts, nor his power, nor his comely proportion. Who can discover the face of his garment? *Or* who can come *to him* with his double bridle? Who can open the doors of his face? His teeth *are* terrible round about. *His* scales *are his* pride, shut up together *as with* a close seal. One is so near to another, that no air can come between them. They are joined one to another, they stick together, that they cannot be sundered. By his sneezing a light doth shine, and his eyes *are* like the eyelids of the morning. Out of his mouth go burning lamps, *and* sparks of fire leap out. Out of his nostrils goeth smoke, as *out* of a seething pot or caldron. His breath kindleth coals, and a flame goeth out of his mouth. In his neck remaineth strength, and sorrow is turned into joy before him. The flakes of his flesh are joined together: they are firm in themselves; they cannot be moved. His heart is as firm as a stone; yea, as hard as a piece of the nether *millstone*. When he raiseth up himself, the mighty are afraid: by reason of breakings they purify themselves. The sword of him that layeth at him cannot hold: the spear, the dart, nor the habergeon. He esteemeth iron as straw, *and* brass as rotten wood. The arrow cannot make him flee: slingstones are turned with him into stubble. Darts are counted as stubble: he laugheth at the shaking of a spear. Sharp stones *are* under him: he spreadeth sharp pointed things upon the mire. He maketh the deep to boil like a pot: he maketh the sea like a pot of ointment. He maketh a path to shine after him; *one* would think the deep *to be* hoary. Upon earth there is not his like, who is made without fear. He beholdeth all high *things:* he *is* a king over all the **children of pride**. *Job 41:1-34*

In Psalm 74 we see God breaking the heads of leviathan. The word for dragon has been translated reptile in some Bibles. In the east some Buddhists and Hindus still worship what is called the Naga, a seven-headed sea serpent.

Thou didst divide the sea by thy strength: thou brakest the heads of the dragons in the waters. Thou brakest the heads of leviathan in pieces, *and* gavest him *to be* meat to the people inhabiting the wilderness. *Psalms 74:13-14*

In Isaiah 27 we see leviathan and the woman that sits on him destroyed. Notice that when this happens, the Nile River will be destroyed. This is referring to the prophecies about the Antichrist destroying three of the ten nations, one of which is Egypt. In this process the Nile River dries up and is destroyed - see *Ancient Prophecies Revealed* for more details.

> In that day the LORD with His sore and great and strong sword shall punish leviathan the piercing serpent, even leviathan that crooked serpent; and He shall slay the dragon that *is* in the sea. In that day sing ye unto her, A vineyard of red wine... And it shall come to pass in that day, *that* the LORD shall beat off from the channel of the river unto the stream of Egypt, and ye shall be gathered one by one, O ye children of Israel. And it shall come to pass in that day, *that* the great trumpet shall be blown, and they shall come which were ready to perish in the land of Assyria, and the outcasts in the land of Egypt, and shall worship the LORD in the holy mount at Jerusalem. *Isaiah 27:1-2, 12-13*

In Ezekiel the Egyptian pharaoh is seen as a type of anti-Israel leviathan.

> Speak, and say, Thus saith the Lord GOD; Behold, I *am* against thee, Pharaoh king of Egypt, the great dragon that lieth in the midst of his rivers, which hath said, My river *is* mine own, and I have made *it* for myself. But I will put hooks in thy jaws, and I will cause the fish of thy rivers to stick unto thy scales, and I will bring thee up out of the midst of thy rivers, and all the fish of thy rivers shall stick unto thy scales. And I will leave thee *thrown* into the wilderness, thee and all the fish of thy rivers: thou shalt fall upon the open fields; thou shalt not be brought together, nor gathered: I have given thee for meat to the beasts of the field and to the fowls of the heaven. *Ezekiel 29:3-5*

This passage goes on to prophesy that all of Egypt will be desolate for forty years.

The Prophet Joel

We can see the timing of the events of the Day of the

Joel 2:1 Rosh Hashanah - Last Trump
Joel 2:11 Yamin Noraim - Days of Awe
Joel 2:15 Yom Kippur - Great Trump

Lord by looking at Joel 2 and his use of festival language. The blowing of the last trump (not the first Pentecost trump) starts the Day of Jehovah which is very terrible (nora) and ends with the blowing of the great shofar at the time of the fast. The Day of Atonement is the only one of the seven festivals that is a fast. It teaches about the Second Coming; see the next chapter for details. This Second Coming is when the bridegroom who has been in the wedding chamber with His bride for one week, leaves with the bride to come to earth. The priests weep between the porch and the altar in the temple and recite the prayer recorded here during the Neilah, or closing part of the service, on the Day of Atonement.

Joel 2: Blow the shofar in Zion, and shout an alarm in My holy mountain. Let all the inhabitants of the land tremble. For the day of Jehovah approaches, it is near; a day of darkness and gloominess, a day of clouds and thick darkness, as the dawn spread out on the mountains, a great and a strong people. There has never been the like, nor shall there ever be again to the years of many generations; a fire devours before them, and a flame burns behind them. The land is as the Garden of Eden before them, and behind them is a desolate wilderness; yea, also nothing shall escape them. Their appearance is like horses; and as horsemen, so they run. They leap on the tops of the mountains with a sound like chariots, like the sound of flames of fire that devour the chaff, as a strong people set in battle array. Before their face the people writhe in pain; all faces gather heat. They run like mighty ones; they go up the wall as men of war. And they each go on his way, and they do not break ranks. And each does not press his brother; they each go in their own paths. And if they fall behind their weapon, they are not cut off. They run to and fro in the city; they run on the wall; they climb up on the houses; they enter in by the windows, like a thief. The earth quakes before them, the heavens tremble. The sun and moon grow dark, and the stars withdraw their brightness. And Jehovah gives His voice before His army, for His camp is very great. For he who does His Word is strong. For the **day of Jehovah is very great** and **terrifying**, and who can endure it? Yet even now turn to Me with all your heart, and with fasting, and with weeping, and with mourning, declares Jehovah. So, tear your heart, and not your garments; and return to Jehovah your God. For He is gracious and merciful, slow to anger, and of great kindness, and He has compassion concerning the evil. Who knows if He will turn and have pity and leave a blessing behind Him, a food offering and a drink offering for Jehovah your God? **Blow the shofar** in Zion, consecrate a **fast**, call a solemn assembly. Gather the people, consecrate the assembly, assemble the elders, gather the children, and those who suck the breasts. **Let the bridegroom go out of his chamber, and the bride out of her room.** Let the priests, the ministers of Jehovah, weep between the porch and the altar; and let them say, **Have compassion on Your people, O Jehovah, and do not give Your possession to reproach, that the nations should rule over them. Why should they say among the peoples, Where is their God?** *Joel 2:1-17*

The 70 Weeks

To draw a good picture of the Days of Awe (the Tribulation period) we must identify the 70th week of Daniel, a period of 2520 days or two sets of 1260 days. In Daniel 9, the angel Gabriel explains that at the end of the 70 weeks of years (490 Jewish years) all would be fulfilled, meaning the Second Coming would occur and Jesus would be anointed king and start His millennial reign.

> "Seventy weeks have been decreed for your people and your holy city, to finish the transgression, to make an end of sin, to make atonement for iniquity, to bring in everlasting righteousness, to seal up vision and prophecy and to anoint the most holy [Jesus Christ]." *Daniel 9:24*

Jesus died at the end of the 69th week, which occurred in AD 32. His death and resurrection began the church age, which fills the gap in the 70-weeks prophecy. About this gap Daniel says:

> "the people of the prince who is to come will destroy the city and the sanctuary. And its end will come with a flood; even to the end there will be war; desolations are determined." *Daniel 9:26*

Here, Daniel describes the period when Titus came and destroyed the Temple. Of this destruction, Jesus prophesied that not one stone would be left upon another. This was fulfilled in AD 70. The last part of verse 26 predicts that the nation of Israel would become desolate. This desolation, or dispersion, took place in stages beginning with the destruction of the Temple in AD 70. The nation was completely dissolved by AD 132. The period of desolation ended when the nation of Israel was reestablished in 1948. So, verse 27 is speaking of the Antichrist during the Tribulation period which occurs sometime after AD 1948.

> "And **he** will make a firm covenant with the many for one week, but in the middle of the week he will put a stop to sacrifice and grain offering; and on the wing of abominations will come one who makes desolate, even until a complete destruction, one that is decreed, is poured out on the one who makes desolate."
> *Daniel 9:27*

In verse 27, the "he" who stops the Temple sacrifices is the Antichrist. Since Jesus returns at the end of the last seven-year period, we know this was not fulfilled by Titus. In order for the Antichrist to *stop* the Temple sacrifices they must be *started* again. In order for the sacrifices to be started, the Jerusalem Temple must be rebuilt. As of AD 2012, this has not occurred. So, some time in the future the Antichrist will confirm, or enforce, a peace covenant with the Jews and Palestinians for a period of seven years. Part of the agreement will permit the Jews to rebuild their Temple.

To this we add the information from 2 Thessalonians 2. Paul here describes the order in which the prophecies will be fulfilled. First, the apostasy comes, then the restrainer leaves, then the Antichrist is revealed by enforcing the peace plan, and finally, the Day of the Lord occurs.

> Now we beseech you, brethren, by the coming of our Lord Jesus Christ, and *by* our gathering together unto him, that ye be not soon shaken in mind, or be troubled, neither by spirit, nor by word, nor by letter as from us, as that the day of Christ is at hand. Let no man deceive you by any means: for *that day shall not*

come, except there come a falling away first, and that man of sin be revealed, the son of perdition; who opposeth and exalteth himself above all that is called God, or that is worshipped; so that he as God sitteth in the temple of God, shewing himself that he is God... For the mystery of iniquity doth already work: only he who now letteth *will let,* until he be taken out of the way. And then shall that Wicked be revealed, whom the Lord shall consume with the spirit of his mouth, and shall destroy with the brightness of his coming: *2 Thessalonians 2:1-4, 7, 8*

Conclusion

The Days of Awe symbolize the seven-year Tribulation period where the Antichrist, leviathan, enforces a peace covenant with Israel and others for a period of seven years, or 2520 days. He is the king of pride and breaks his covenant halfway into the seven years. He destroys Egypt and slaughters many nations. Many details about him are given in the book of Revelation. He will be destroyed by the Second Coming of the Messiah to earth when He establishes His messianic kingdom.

7-Year Tribulation

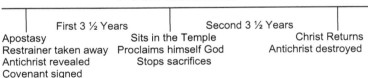

First 3 ½ Years	Second 3 ½ Years	
Apostasy	Sits in the Temple	Christ Returns
Restrainer taken away	Proclaims himself God	Antichrist destroyed
Antichrist revealed	Stops sacrifices	
Covenant signed		

Day of Atonement, Yom Kippur

ים כיפור

Tishrei						
S	M	T	W	T	F	S
					1	2
3	4	5	6	7	8	9
10	11	12	13	14	15	16
17	18	19	20	21	22	23
24	25	26	27	28	29	30

Also on the tenth *day* of this seventh month *there shall be* a day of atonement: it shall be a holy convocation unto you; and ye shall afflict your souls, and offer an offering made by fire unto the LORD. And ye shall do no work in that same day: for it *is* a day of atonement, to make an atonement for you before the LORD your God... in the ninth *day* of the month at even, from even unto even, shall ye celebrate your sabbath. *Leviticus 23:27-28,32*

This festival teaches about the Second Coming of the Messiah, and the destruction of the Antichrist.

The Great Trump
The Festival of Trumpets is called the Festival of "The Awakening Blast" and the "Last Trump." In contrast with this, the festival of the Day of Atonement is called the "Festival of the *Great* Trump." This helps us organize the

prophecies in Scripture. Whenever we see "last trump" in Scripture, we know it is referring to the time of the Rapture/Resurrection of believers. Whenever we see the "great trump" we know it is referring to the Second Coming. To verify the different festival names, look them up in the Encyclopedia Judaica.

Look in Joel. This trump is blown on *the* fast. The only fast on a festival is the Day of Atonement. So we know it is the great trump. This is the day that the Lord comes out of His bridal chamber (He has been with the church for seven years) and the day the priests minister between the porch and the altar. The prayer that they speak here is part of the required prayer still recited during the Day of Atonement ritual.

> Blow the trumpet in Zion, sanctify a fast, call a solemn assembly: gather the people, sanctify the congregation, assemble the elders, gather the children, and those that suck the breasts: let the bridegroom go forth of his chamber, and the bride out of her closet. Let the priests, the ministers of the LORD, weep between the porch and the altar, and let them say, Spare thy people, O LORD, and give not thine heritage to reproach, that the heathen should rule over them: wherefore should they say among the people, Where *is* their God? *Joel 2:15-17*

In Matthew 24 Jesus stated that at the great trump, or Yom Kippur, people would see His return and His angels would gather the elect (those believers who made it though the Tribulation alive) to Jerusalem for His coronation. People often misinterpret this passage as the Rapture of the church, which leads to falsely believing in a post-tribulation Rapture.

And then shall appear the sign of the Son of man in heaven: and then shall all the tribes of the earth mourn, and they shall see the Son of Man coming in the clouds of heaven with power and great glory. And he shall send his angels with a great sound of a trumpet, and they shall gather together his elect from the four winds, from one end of heaven to the other. *Matthew 24:30-31*

Ritual of Two Goats
During the festival of Yom Kippur there is a prophetic ceremony that involves two goats. Two nearly identical goats are selected and brought before the high priest. The high priest places his hands on one of the goats. Another priest brings out the *Qalephi*, a box containing two lots. One of the lots is randomly withdrawn by the high priest and placed with the first goat. Then the other is withdrawn for the second goat. On one lot is engraved לאדני, meaning "for the Lord." The goat that randomly acquired the lot "for the Lord" is sacrificed for the sins of the people. This animal is a perfect representation of the Messiah dying for the sins of the world. The other lot is engraved with לעזאזל, meaning "for Azazel." This has commonly been translated "scapegoat," but Azazel actually is a proper name. Moses wrote about this ceremony in Leviticus 16 saying:

And Aaron shall cast lots upon the two goats; one lot for the LORD, and the other lot for the scapegoat. And Aaron shall bring the goat upon which the LORD'S lot fell, and offer him for a sin offering. But the goat, on which the lot fell to be the scapegoat, shall be presented alive before the LORD, to make an atonement with him, and to let him go <u>for a scapegoat</u> [to Azazel] into the wilderness. *Leviticus 16:8-10*

The Mishnah is a book written about AD 200. It contains the Oral Torah, or the exact details explaining how to perform the rituals described in the Old Testament. In Yoma 4.2 of the Mishnah, details are given concerning the ceremony of the two goats.

A scarlet-colored wool cord was specially created for this ceremony. One piece of this cord was tied to one of the horns of the Azazel goat. One piece of the cord was tied around the neck of the Lord's goat.

Leviticus describes the Azazel goat being sent into the "wilderness." But the Mishnah gives greater detail about that part of the ritual in Yoma 6. The two goats must be alike in appearance, size, and weight. The "wilderness" that the Azazel goat was taken to was actually a ravine twelve miles east of Jerusalem. Between Jerusalem and this ravine were ten stations or booths. Since it was a High Holy Day, one could not travel very far. One priest took the Azazel goat from Jerusalem to the first booth. Then another priest took it from the second to the third booth. This continued until a priest took it from the tenth booth to the ravine. Anciently this ravine was called Beit HaDudo. It still exists in the Judean desert and is presently called Jabel Muntar. The Mishnah then says the priest took the crimson cord off of the goat and tied one piece to the large rock on the cliff of the ravine, and he tied the other piece back on to the horns of the goat. He then pushed the goat off the cliff. Before it would be halfway down the cliff, it was already torn into pieces.

If the ritual was properly done, the crimson cord would turn snow white. At that point the priest would signal the tenth booth, which would in turn signal the ninth, all the way back to the first booth, which would signal the high priest standing at the door of the sanctuary. When the high priest learned the crimson thread had turned white, he finished the ritual by quoting the prophet Isaiah.

"'Come now, and let us reason together,' saith the LORD: 'though your sins be as scarlet, they shall be as white as snow; though they be red like crimson, they shall be as wool.'" *Isaiah 1:18*

Then a massive celebration began.

The Meaning of the Ritual

It has been speculated that the scapegoat represents Jesus taking away our sin. That is one possible interpretation. If the information given in the Mishnah is correct, another picture emerges. Two identical goats, one dedicated to God, the other dedicated to Satan. One goat represents the Messiah and the other represents the Antichrist. The only way to tell the difference between the Messiah and the Antichrist is to know the Lord's will by carefully studying the Word of God. At the Second Coming, the Antichrist will be destroyed in Megiddo, in a battle called Armageddon.

Miracles Stopped

In the Babylonian Talmud, Yoma 40a states that three miracles occurred connected with the festivals. First, the scarlet cord of the Azazel goat would turn white at his death; second, the gates of the Temple would close by themselves at the end of the Neilah portion of the Day of Atonement ritual; and third, the Angel troubled the water (see the chapter on the Great Salvation). The Talmud states these miracles suddenly stopped occurring for some unknown reason about forty years prior to the destruction of the second temple in AD 70. Forty years prior to the destruction of the second temple would be the time the Messiah died fulfilling the prophecies!

The Rest of the Ritual

Now with the rejoicing in Azazel's death, the High Priest moved forward with the rest of the ceremony. The High Priest removed the innards of the bull and the goat whose blood had been sprinkled in the Holy of Holies and placed them in a receptacle. He twisted the bodies of the two animals and four priests carried the bodies out of Jerusalem on two poles to a place called "the place of the ashes... where the bull and goat were burned only after the Azazel goat had reached the wilderness. The High Priest went into the Court of the Women and read Leviticus 16:23, 27-32; and recited by heart Numbers 29:7-11.

Following this recitation of Scripture, a number of prayers were pronounced by the High Priest. Then he recited eight benedictions: for the Torah, for the (sacrificial) service, for the thanksgiving, for the forgiving of sins, for the Temple separately, for Israel separately, for Jerusalem separately, for the Kohanim (priests) separately, and for other matters of prayer.

The High Priest then returned to the roof of the Beit Haparvah (a chamber in the temple) to remove his linen garments. He then immersed himself in the bath and put on the golden garments. He washed his hands and feet before removing one set of garments and after putting on the other. Immediately, he went to the north side of the altar, where he offered up his ram and a ram for the people as burnt offerings. Next he performed all the principle parts of the ordinary evening sacrifices. He also burned the innards previously removed from the bull and goat.

The Closing of the Gates - Neilah

The last ritual of the Day of Atonement is the "closing of the gates." This corresponds to the opening of the gates for the Rapture / Resurrection at Rosh Hashanah, when the believers are taken away. If the sinners who go though the Tribulation period have not repented by the time of the closing of the gates (the Second Coming) their names will be added to the Book of Death and they will become the wicked, or the *rashim*.

Deuteronomy 15:1-2 states that every seven years on the Day of Atonement, all debts are forgiven for Israelites but not for unbelievers or foreigners. This is a picture that at the end of the seven-year Tribulation those who have become believers in Messiah are forgiven of their sins, but those who have not been forgiven are judged. Jesus told of this in his parable of the Sheep and Goat Judgment in Matthew 25.

Day of Redemption - Yom HaPeduth
Another name for the Day of Atonement is *Yom HaPeduth*, or the Day of Redemption. This title teaches that the earth is redeemed on this day. The resurrected come back to take the kingdom. The ones left on the earth are judged on this day. Jesus talked about this in the parable of the sheep and the goats in Matthew 25. The apostle Paul referred to this day in Ephesians:

And grieve not the Holy Spirit of God, whereby ye are sealed unto the day of redemption. *Ephesians 4:30*

Face to Face
On this one day of the year, the high priest went past the veil into the Holy of Holies and met with God face to face. Paul used this Yom Kippur phrase in 1 Corinthians 13 indicating that the gifts and prophecies will be complete when we see Jesus begin His rule on earth on a future Yom Kippur.

For now we see through a glass, darkly; but then face to face: now I know in part; but then shall I know even as also I am known. *1 Corinthians 13:12*

The prophet Zechariah taught on this day Jesus' feet would literally touch down on the Mount of Olives and He would cross over to Jerusalem to become king. The Mount of Olives will split in two.

And His feet shall stand in that day upon the mount of Olives, which *is* before Jerusalem on the east, and the Mount of Olives shall cleave in the midst thereof toward the east and toward the west, *and there shall be* a very great valley; and half of the mountain shall remove toward the north, and half of it toward the south. *Zechariah 14:4*

Other Ancient Sources
Barnabas 7 describes the same Azazel ritual but uses the name Rachia for the cliff called Beit Hadudo. Barnabas then explains that the two goats point to the two comings of the Messiah. Justin Martyr agrees with Barnabas's interpretation of the two goats symbolizing the two comings of the Messiah.

Enoch 10, 54, and 55 seem to indicate that Azazel represents the Antichrist in the last days. Azazel (the Antichrist) and all "those who follow him" are ritually bound under Beit Hadudo when the Azazel goat is thrown over the cliff. Compare this to when Satan is bound for the thousand years.

Biblical events that occurred on the Day of Atonement
Release all debt every seven years
Second Coming

Tabernacles, Sukkot

סוכות

Tishrei						
S	M	T	W	T	F	S
					1	2
3	4	5	6	7	8	9
10	11	12	13	14	15	16
17	18	19	20	21	22	23
24	25	26	27	28	29	30

Speak unto the children of Israel, saying, The fifteenth day of this seventh month *shall be* the feast of tabernacles *for* seven days unto the LORD. On the first day *shall be* an holy convocation: ye shall do no servile work *therein*. Seven days ye shall offer an offering made by fire unto the LORD: on the eighth day shall be an holy convocation unto you; and ye shall offer an offering made by fire unto the LORD: it *is* a solemn assembly; *and* ye shall do no servile work *therein. Leviticus 23:34-36*

The festival of Tabernacles teaches us about the millennial reign. It is called "the season of our joy," taken from the word rejoice in Leviticus 23:4. It is also called the "Festival of Ingathering." Whenever a passage just says a "festival," it is *Sukkot*, the most important festival of the Jews.

It is called the "Festival of Ingathering," because it begins with a great supper. The Israelites would take the second tithe and prepare a great feast. This happened every three years on the festival of Tabernacles. See Deuteronomy 14 for details.

In the Temple seventy burnt offerings were given for the cleansing of all the Gentile nations (Numbers 29). Based on this passage the rabbis called this festival "The Festival of Nations."

Four Species
On the first day of Tabernacles, each man was to bring what is called the four species.

> And ye shall take you on the first day the boughs [fruit] of goodly trees, branches of palm trees, and the boughs of thick [myrtle] trees, and willows of the brook; and ye shall rejoice before the LORD your God seven days. *Leviticus 23:40*

The *Lulov* is made with a tall palm branch in the center, a myrtle branch on one side, and a willow branch on the other side. These are bound together and held in the right hand. The fruit spoken of here is an etrog or yellow citron. It grows on a tree that produces fruit all year long. The fruit juice is often mixed with wine as an antidote for consuming poison.

The ritual consisted of holding the four species, the Lulov, in the right hand representing the Messiah, and the etrog upside down in the left hand, representing the Israelite and the world, backwards in sin. By the end of the ritual the etrog is right side up and joined in marriage to the Lulovim, creating the four species.

The Sukkah

Each Israelite family builds a tabernacle or tent, called a *sukkah*, out of the branches of palm, willow, myrtle, and other trees. They live in it for seven days.

And ye shall take you on the first day the boughs of goodly trees, branches of palm trees, and the boughs of thick trees, and willows of the brook; and ye shall rejoice before the LORD your God seven days. And ye shall keep it a feast unto the LORD seven days in the year. *It shall be* a statute for ever in your generations: ye shall celebrate it in the seventh month. Ye shall dwell in booths seven days; all that are Israelites born shall dwell in booths: that your generations may know that I made the children of Israel to dwell in booths, when I brought them out of the land of Egypt: I *am* the LORD your God. *Leviticus 23:40-43*

Three Stars

One rabbinical requirement was that there be an opening in the roof of the sukkah large enough for the family members to see three stars. Genesis states we are to pay attention to the sun, moon, and stars for signs, *moedim* [seasons], and for calendar purposes [days and years].

And God said, Let there be lights in the firmament of the heaven to divide the day from the night; and let them be for signs, and for seasons, and for days, and years: *Genesis 1:14*

If we use the proper calendar as described in the first chapter, we can accurately calculate the festivals and their future events. The star of Bethlehem is one example of a sign in the heavens.

Ushpizin

Each day you are to have a meal with your family in the sukkah. An extra place is set for a guest. One night it is for Abraham, the next night for Isaac, then Jacob and so on. This rehearsal teaches us that in the millennium mortals and immortals will dwell together.

> Let us be glad and rejoice, and give honour to Him: for the marriage of the Lamb is come, and His wife hath made herself ready. And to her was granted that she should be arrayed in fine linen, clean and white: for the fine linen is the righteousness of saints. And he saith unto me, write, blessed *are* they which are called unto the marriage supper of the Lamb. And he saith unto me, These are the true sayings of God. *Revelation 19:7-9*

This great supper is the marriage supper of the Lamb and is in contrast to the feast of Leviathan.

The Feast of Leviathan

According to the Encyclopedia Judaica, Leviathan was anciently thought to be a seven-headed sea beast. It represents the Antichrist and his end time kingdom.

The Feast of Leviathan is taken from Job 41.

> Canst thou draw out leviathan with an hook? Shall the companions make a banquet of him? *Job 41:1,6*

Those who follow Leviathan will be slaughtered in the battle of Armageddon. Their flesh will be for the birds to feast on. This has also been applied to the Sheep and Goat Judgment of Matthew 25.

> And I saw an angel standing in the sun; and he cried with a loud voice, saying to all the fowls that fly in the midst of heaven, Come and gather yourselves together unto the supper of the great God; that ye may eat the flesh of kings, and the flesh of captains, and the flesh of mighty men, and the flesh of horses, and of them that sit on them, and the flesh of all *men, both* free and bond, both small and great.
> *Revelation 19:17-18*

References to Leviathan in Scripture are found in Job 41; Isaiah 27, 42; Ezekiel 29; and Psalms 104, 72, 74. He is also referred to as the Tannin, or twisted serpent, and Rehab, which is a Hebrew word for pride. See Job 9:13, Isaiah 51:9; and Isaiah 30.

When the Egyptians were drowned in the sea, their bodies were left for the birds; likewise the bodies of those destroyed in the battle of Armageddon will be left as food for the birds. While the church has the Marriage Supper of the Lamb, the unbelievers will take part in the Banquet of Leviathan.

Jesus says at the great trump the angels will gather the people, taking the sheep back to Jerusalem and the goats to where the eagles gather, or the Feast of Leviathan.

Matthew 24:28; Luke 17:37

> Two *men* shall be in the field; the one shall be taken, and the other left. And they answered and said unto him, Where, Lord? And he said unto them, Wheresoever the body *is,* thither will the eagles be gathered together. *Luke 17:36-37*

House of the Water Pouring - Beit HaShoevah

Beit HaShoevah is a ritual that was performed every day during Sukkot. A group of priests would gather together and go out the Eastern Gate to the Mount of Olives and from there to a valley called Motzah. They would cut willow branches, each about twenty-five feet long. The priests would then make a precession back to the temple waving the willow branches. This would create the sound of a mighty rushing wind.

While this was going on, the high priest and an assistant would leave the temple, going out through the Water Gate down to the pool of Siloam also called Siloah. The high priest would fill a golden vessel with living water from the pool and take it back to the temple. The high priest timed his reentering through the Water Gate with the procession of priests carrying the willow branches returning though the Eastern Gate. This is a prophecy that when the Messiah returns, He will come though the Eastern Gate. At that time the shofar was blown and a single flute began to play. The man playing the flute is called "the pierced one." This was to signal both groups had returned and were about to enter the temple. At that moment another group of priests ascended the altar and began the additional animal sacrifices for that day of Sukkot.

Then the procession of priests would march around the altar seven times and lay the willow branches against the altar to form what looks like a sukkah over it. This canopy is called a "chuppah," or wedding canopy. Then the high priest with his golden vessel of living water and his assistant with his silver vessel of sacred wine would ascend the altar and pour both liquids together over the altar to cleanse it. At that moment the crowd witnessing this ritual would sing Isaiah 12:3.

And in that day Thou shalt say, O LORD, I will praise Thee: though Thou wast angry with me, Thine anger is turned away, and Thou comfortedst me. Behold, God *is* my salvation [Yehsua]; I will trust, and not be afraid: for the LORD JEHOVAH *is* my strength and *my* song; He also is become my salvation. Therefore with joy shall ye draw water out of the wells of salvation [Yeshua]. And in that day shall ye say, Praise the LORD, call upon His name, declare His doings among the people, make mention that His name is exalted. Sing unto the LORD; for He hath done excellent things: this *is* known in all the earth. Cry out and shout, thou inhabitant of Zion: for great *is* the Holy One of Israel in the midst of thee.
Isaiah 12:1-6

Note that the word "salvation" here is "Yeshua" – the Hebrew name of Jesus.

The last day of Sukkot was called "the Great Day," Hoshana Rabbah. It was most likely at the time of the water pouring that Jesus stood up and said:

In the last day, that great *day* of the feast, Jesus stood and cried, saying, If any man thirst, let him come unto me, and drink. He that believeth on me, as the scripture hath said, out of his belly shall flow rivers of living water. (But this spake He of the Spirit, which they that believe on Him should receive: for the Holy Ghost was not yet *given;* because that Jesus was not yet glorified.) *John 7:37-39*

The ceremony of the Biet HaShoevah teaches about the Messianic Kingdom, the birth of the Messiah, the dedication of the temple, and the pouring of living water (water and wine) to cleanse the temple. Note Jesus' first miracle was to turn the water into wine and He used the large stone pots that were designed for this ceremony to hold the sacred wine. Jesus turned normal water into sacred wine (or living water) showing that He was the fulfillment of this ceremony.

Zechariah predicted that all nations will be required to keep the Festival of Tabernacles, called the Festival of the Nations, during the Millennium.

> And it shall come to pass, *that* every one that is left of all the nations which came against Jerusalem shall even go up from year to year to worship the King, the LORD of hosts, and to keep the feast of tabernacles.
> *Zechariah 14:16*

Jesus' Birth

Jesus was born on the first day of the feast of Tabernacles. John referenced this when he used the Greek word skēnoō (Strong's 4637) meaning "to dwell." It comes from the root word skēnē (Strong's 4633) which means tabernacle. John literally said Jesus "tabernacled among us."

> And the Word was made flesh, and <u>dwelt</u> [tabernacled] among us, (and we beheld his glory, the glory as of the only begotten of the Father,) full of grace and truth.
> *John 1:14*

Jesus was born in an animal stable. In Genesis 33:17 we see Jacob built a stable for his animals. This same word used in that passage is the word used for a sukkah or booth used on the Festival of Tabernacles.

We know Jesus' birth was not in the cold of winter because the shepherds would not have had their sheep out in the cold. They kept them in caves and stables in the winter. So He was not born on December 25.

And there were in the same country shepherds abiding in the field, keeping watch over their flock by night. *Luke 2:8*

When the angels appeared with glory lighting up the night sky, they announced glad tidings of great joy for all people. Sukkot is called the "Season of Our Joy" and the "Festival of Lights." Sukkot is also the "Festival of the Nations" or for all people. They said the sign would be the Messiah was lying in a sukkah (manger) wrapped in swaddling clothes. Swaddling clothes are normal for a baby; so why was this a sign? The old swaddling cloths (or undergarments of the priests) were used as wicks for the sixteen great lights used during the Festival of Lights which was going on in the temple at that very moment! This showed that the Light of the World was just born and that he was a Melchizedekian priest dressed in priestly garb. Angels lit up the night sky on this Festival of Lights to announce the birth of the Light of the World.

We determined in the chapter on Passover that John the Baptist was born on the Festival of Passover. Luke 1 tells us that Jesus was born six months later. This would place His conception around Hanukah and therefore His birth, nine months later, would fall around the first of Tabernacles.

And after those days his wife Elisabeth conceived, and hid herself five months, saying, Thus hath the Lord dealt with me in the days wherein he looked on *me*, to take away my reproach among men. And in the sixth month the angel Gabriel was sent from God unto a city of Galilee, named Nazareth, to a virgin espoused to a man whose name was Joseph, of the house of David; and the virgin's name *was* Mary... And, behold, thy cousin Elisabeth, she hath also conceived a son in her old age: and this is the sixth month with her... *Luke 1:24-27, 36*

When the angel Gabriel came to Mary to announce she was to be the mother of the Messiah, Mary was saying the traditional prayers for the season of Hanukah. The phrase "behold the handmaiden of the Lord," recorded in Luke 1:38, is part of those prayers. So Luke 1 shows the time of the conception to be Kislev or December, which placed the birth of Jesus around the Feast of Tabernacles.

The Roman decree commanding Jews to travel to their home cities for the census would not have occurred in the winter, either, but most likely in the fall after all the crops were harvested and taxes could be paid.

And it came to pass in those days, that there went out a decree from Caesar Augustus, that all the world should be taxed. *(And* this taxing was first made when Cyrenius was governor of Syria.) And all went to be taxed, every one into his own city. And Joseph also went up from Galilee, out of the city of Nazareth, into Judaea, unto the city of David, which is called Bethlehem; (because he was of the house and lineage of David:) *Luke 2:1-4*

Most Jews traveled to Jerusalem on Tabernacles for the Jewish festival when they paid the last tithe from the fall crops.

Jesus was baptized on his thirtieth birthday (when he began to be thirty) by John the Baptist.

And Jesus himself began to be about thirty years of age, being (as was supposed) the son of Joseph, which was *the son* of Heli, *Luke 3:23*

Jesus was baptized (Matthew 3:15) as a Melchizedekian priest (Psalm 110:4; Hebrews 5:8-10; 6:20). Jesus became the sacrifice for our sin (1 Pet. 2:24; 2 Cor. 5:21) in His role as a priest. To be consecrated as a priest, Jesus had to be baptized (Lev. 8:6; Exodus 29:4, Matt. 3:16) and anointed with oil – the Holy Spirit – (Leviticus 8:12; Exodus 29:7; Matthew 3:16). One could not be become a priest until the age of thirty (Numbers 4:3).

We read in John's Gospel that Jesus was baptized into priesthood (1:29-34), then we see a Passover occur (2:13-25), then Jesus talked to the Samaritan woman four months before the harvest festival or Pentecost (4:35). This means almost a year had passed since the last Passover. Then a Tabernacles occurred (5:1-15), then a Passover (6:1-15), then a Tabernacles (7:1-24), then a Hanukah (10:22-42), then the Passover on which He was crucified (11:45-57). So we conclude Jesus had a three-and-a-half-year ministry.

We know Jesus' birthday had to be before winter weather could have set in and the Father would have not have let Him be born around Halloween (see Chapter on Halloween) which puts it before October / Chesvan. We know He had a three-and-a-half-year ministry which ended in the spring on Passover and began when He was baptized into the priesthood on His thirtieth birthday by John the Baptist. Exactly six months prior to Passover is the start of Tabernacles. Finally, we also have John stating that Jesus "tabernacled among us."

This does not absolutely prove Jesus was born on Tabernacles; but based on all the other festival language and embedded prophecy, this fits the rituals perfectly. The main symbolism is that Jesus, the King, was born on the festival that teaches about the Messianic Kingdom!

The Great Salvation, The Great Day

Tishrei						
S	M	T	W	T	F	S
					1	2
3	4	5	6	7	8	9
10	11	12	13	14	15	16
17	18	19	20	21	22	23
24	25	26	27	28	29	30

The Eighth day after Tabernacles is called *Hoshana Rabbah*, meaning "the great salvation." This is Tishrei 21. This high Sabbath teaches about the end of the Messianic Kingdom, the new heavens and earth, and the beginning of eternity.

> Speak unto the children of Israel, saying, The fifteenth day of this seventh month *shall be* the feast of tabernacles *for* seven days unto the LORD. On the first day *shall be* an holy convocation: ye shall do no servile work *therein*. Seven days ye shall offer an offering made by fire unto the LORD: on the eighth day shall be an holy convocation unto you; and ye shall offer an offering made by fire unto the LORD: it *is* a solemn assembly; *and* ye shall do no servile work *therein. Leviticus 23:34-36*

The Four Species

On Hoshana Rabbah the ritual of the four species is preformed, but this time the participants circle the altar seven times instead of just once. During Sukkot the ritual is focused on the Messiah restoring His kingdom to earth (the Millennium) but now with seven times in a row, the focus is restoring the earth, and the coming of the New Jerusalem. During this time Psalm 26 is read.

A Psalm of **David.** Judge me, O LORD; for I have walked in mine integrity: I have trusted also in the LORD; *therefore* I shall not slide. Examine me, O LORD, and prove me; try my reins and my heart. For Thy lovingkindness *is* before mine eyes: and I have walked in Thy truth. I have not sat with vain persons, neither will I go in with dissemblers. I have hated the congregation of evil doers; and will not sit with the wicked. I will wash mine hands in innocency: so will I compass Thine altar, O LORD: that I may publish with the voice of thanksgiving, and tell of all Thy wondrous works. LORD, I have loved the habitation of Thy house, and the place where Thine honour dwelleth. Gather not my soul with sinners, nor my life with bloody men: in whose hands *is* mischief, and their right hand is full of bribes. But as for me, I will walk in mine integrity: redeem me, and be merciful unto me. My foot standeth in an even place: in the congregations will I bless the LORD. *Psalms 26:1-12*

Rejoicing of the House of the Water Pouring
Simchat Beit HaShoevah

The same ritual of the House of the Water Pouring was done with the exception that when Isaiah 12 is sung, each verse would be preceded by the words "Hoshana" meaning "Save now," or "please save," and that evening there would be singing and dancing. Some of the priestly dancers would have wands of fire that they twirled around in celebration of the Light of the World.

The theme of this festival is the final judgment. It teaches about the final rebellion of Gog and Magog and the Great White Throne judgment.

It is customary to read the whole of Tehillim (Psalms) on Hoshana Rabbah eve. There is also a custom to read the book of Deuteronomy on the night of Hoshana Rabbah.

Jesus is the Living Water
Jesus set the stage for His teaching about the living water by doing His first miracle at a wedding in Cana, where He turned the water into wine. The key to understanding why He did that is that He used sacred water pots for His miracle.

> And there were set there six water pots of stone, after the manner of the purifying of the Jews, containing two or three firkins apiece. *John 2:6*

These were the water pots used for the purification ceremony in the temple on Hoshana Rabbah. In the second year of His ministry (John 4), Jesus told the Samaritan woman that He was the Messiah and that only He had the "living water." Jesus was on His way to Jerusalem for the feast. In John 5, Jesus arrived at the feast and healed the man waiting for the angel.

> After this there was a feast of the Jews; and Jesus went up to Jerusalem. Now there is at Jerusalem by the sheep *market* a pool, which is called in the Hebrew tongue Bethesda, having five porches. In these lay a great multitude of impotent folk, of blind, halt, withered, waiting for the moving of the water. For an angel went down at a certain season into the pool, and troubled the water: whosoever then first

after the troubling of the water stepped in was made whole of whatsoever disease he had. *John 5:1-4*

The pools of Bethsaida and Siloam were mikvas, or baptismals, for the ancient Jews and used heavily by pilgrims during the festivals of Passover, Pentecost, and Tabernacles. God would send an angel to one or both of these pools and trouble the water. At that time the first person to go into the water was healed. When this healing miracle occurred it showed that God had created living water for the healing of the nations. This healing water would then be collected for the purification rituals of Sukkot and the ashes of the Red Heifer.

All Miracles Stopped When the Messiah Came

Remember we said that according to the Talmud, Yoma 40a, three miracles always occurred during the Fall Holy days? The crimson cord tied around the Azazel goat would

Miracles that Ceased
Temple gates opening
Temple gates closing
Temple light staying lit
Scarlett cord turning white
Angel troubling the water

turn white; the temple doors would shut by themselves; and the angel would trouble the water. Yoma 40a actually states that these three miracles stopped happening about forty years before the destruction of the second temple in AD 70. This would have been during the Messiah's ministry. I personally believe that the last time the angel troubled the water was the year before Jesus healed the sick man. The angel pointed to Christ.

Later in the temple, Jesus was seen teaching that He was the fulfillment of the living water, the manna from heaven, and many other symbols.

In the last day, that great *day* of the feast, Jesus stood and cried, saying, If any man thirst, let him come unto

Me, and drink. He that believeth on Me, as the scripture hath said, out of his belly shall flow rivers of living water. (But this spake He of the Spirit, which they that believe on Him should receive: for the Holy Ghost was not yet *given;* because that Jesus was not yet glorified.) *John 7:37-39*

The Eighth Conclusion, Shimini Atzeret

שמיני עצרת

Tishrei						
S	M	T	W	T	F	S
					1	2
3	4	5	6	7	8	9
10	11	12	13	14	15	16
17	18	19	20	21	22	23
24	25	26	27	28	29	30

Also in the fifteenth day of the seventh month, when ye have gathered in the fruit of the land, ye shall keep a feast unto the LORD seven days: on the first day *shall be* a sabbath, and on the eighth day *shall be* a sabbath. *Leviticus 23:39*

The Eighth Conclusion or *Shimini Azteret* is on Tisrei 22. It is a two-day festival teaching about eternity. The world to come, the Olam Haba, will begin with the descent of the New Jerusalem.

Jesus' Circumcision
God commanded that each baby boy was to be circumcised on the eighth day after birth. Since Jesus was born on the first day of the festival of Tabernacles, His circumcision was done properly, according to the Law of

Moses, eight days later on the Festival of the Eighth Conclusion.

> And when the days of her purification according to the law of Moses were accomplished, they brought Him to Jerusalem, to present *Him* to the Lord; (as it is written in the law of the Lord, every male that openeth the womb shall be called holy to the Lord;) *Luke 2:22-23*

Writing in the Dust

In John 8:2 we see Jesus entering the temple the day after the Great day. This would have been the twenty-second or Shimini Azteret. They brought to Him a woman caught in adultery. In the preceding days the rabbis would have taught about all the verses in Scripture that referenced the living water. Jesus taught He was the living water during this time. One of these living water passages was in Jeremiah.

> O LORD, the hope of Israel, all that forsake thee shall be ashamed, *and* they that depart from Me shall be written in the earth, because they have forsaken the LORD, the fountain of living waters. *Jeremiah 17:13*

When Jesus said "whoever is without sin may cast the first stone," and they all just stood there. Jesus then bent down and wrote their names in the dirt. This meant by rejecting His authority, they were rejecting the living water and when He wrote their names in the earth they were damned. They all immediately fled.

> So when they continued asking Him, He lifted up Himself, and said unto them, He that is without sin among you, let him first cast a stone at her. And again He stooped down, and wrote on the ground. And they

which heard *it,* being convicted by *their own* conscience, went out one by one, beginning at the eldest, *even* unto the last: and Jesus was left alone, and the woman standing in the midst. *John 8:7-9*

Simchat Torah

Simchat Torah occurs on Tishrei 23. However, just like Rosh Hashanah it is considered one long 48-hour day, Shimini Azteret along with Simchat Torah is considered to be two parts of one long 48-hour day.

On Simchat Torah the Jews complete their annual cycle of Torah readings and start again from *Bereshit* (Genesis). Simchat Torah is considered to be a time of "fulfillment" of the Torah. The circumcision of Yeshua (Jesus) at this time indicates how He had come to fulfill the Law and the Prophets (Matthew 5:17-18).

Other Prophetic Ceremonies

Hanukkah

הנוכה

Kislev						
S	M	T	W	T	F	S
	1	2	3	4	5	6
7	8	9	10	11	12	13
14	15	16	17	18	19	20
21	22	23	24	25	26	27
28	29	30				

Tevet						
S	M	T	W	T	F	S
			1	2	3	4
5	6	7	8	9	10	11
12	13	14	15	16	17	18
19	20	21	22	23	24	25
26	27	28	29			

The Festival of Hanukkah commemorates the time when the Maccabees took back Jerusalem from the Syrians in 165 BC. This story is recorded in 1 Maccabees. It is celebrated from Kislev 25 until Tevet 2, eight days total.

It is called the Festival of Lights, the Feast of Dedication, and is sometimes referred to as the Second Tabernacles.

Antiochus Epiphanies was the ruler of the Seleucid Empire in Syria. He demanded to be worshiped as God and placed an idol in the holy place of the Jerusalem temple and sacrificed a pig on the altar.

> On Kislev (Nov.-Dec.) 25, 168 [BC], the "abomination of desolation" (Dan. xi. 31, xii. 11) was set up on the altar of burnt offering in the temple, and the Jews required to make obeisance to it.
> *Jewishencyclopedia.com - Antiochus IV., Epiphanes*

The Talmud records that when the Maccabees regained control of the Temple Mount, they cleansed it and rededicated it; but there was only enough oil in the temple to last for one day. It normally takes eight days to make the oil in the manner prescribed by Scripture. God performed a miracle and caused the light to burn for eight days on that one day's worth of oil. This is why the festival of Hanukkah is celebrated for eight days.

The Talmud also adds that the light's nonstop burning ceased about forty years before the destruction of the Second Temple. This would have been the time of the Messiah's First Coming.

The first time we see Hanukkah in Scripture is in the prophecies of Daniel 11 where he predicts the abomination of desolation and the revolt of the Maccabees. Jesus gave a speech in the temple on one Hanukkah.

> And it was at Jerusalem the feast of the dedication, and it was winter. And Jesus walked in the temple in Solomon's porch. *John 10:22-23*

In contrast to Antiochus Epiphanies claiming to be god and killing those who refused to believe in him, Jesus said He truly is God incarnate and He will give eternal live to all those who trust in Him and they will never die. No one is strong enough to take them out of His hand!

This festival teaches us that the Antichrist will set up the image (abomination) in the holy place in the temple like Antiochus did. He will also come to power as Antiochus did.

Antiochus Epiphanes "seized" the "honor of kingship" (Daniel 11) from his brother Demetrius I, and had Onias III, the 'prince of the covenant" assassinated. See 2 Maccabees 4:4-10. Antiochus Epiphanes deceived Rome into officially recognizing him. He attacked Egypt and a rumor started in Israel that he was dead. This greatly angered him. He went back northwest to Israel and entered the temple and defiled it in 168 BC. See 1 Maccabees 1:19-20. Antiochus polluted the sanctuary by forbidding the daily sacrifice to be offered and by placing his idol, the abomination, in the holy place of the temple, making the whole temple desolate. He occupied Jerusalem for three and a half years before he was driven out by the Maccabees.

Revelation states the false prophet will call down fire from heaven like the two witnesses will do, and he will place an idol in the temple just as Antiochus did.

New Moon

ראש קודש

S	M	T	W	T	F	S
					1	2
3	4	5	6	7	8	9
10	11	12	13	14	15	16
17	18	19	20	21	22	23
24	25	26	27	28		

The first day of a Jewish month always begins on a new moon. The middle or fifteenth of the month is a full moon. The new moon is called *Rosh Kodesh*. This literally means the head or beginning of the holy. It is called the Festival of the Born Again because the moon has gone through its cycle of birth to fullness to death and is now reborn anew.

The prophets would often receive their visions on the new moon. (See Ezekiel 26:1, 29:17, 31:1, Haggai 1:1) Many would seek out a prophet on the new moon to inquire of the Lord. (See 2 Kings 4:23).

Church Apostasy and Rapture
In the beginning Israel knew almost nothing about God (a new moon) but Moses and the prophets led them into a fuller knowledge of Him (full moon). In time, the nation apostatized back into unbelief (new moon) not reflecting God's light into the world. Then revivals came and the

cycle repeated itself. This is one reason why the New Moon festival is called the Festival of the Born Again.

The New Moon festival likewise teaches that the church grew in knowledge though the Holy Spirit (new moon to a full moon) and it is now waning back into apostasy (new moon). Once the apostasy is complete, the remaining true believers will be Raptured (or concealed away) before the Tribulation begins.

It was also customary for the husband and wife to get away on the New Moon. Alone time, once a month, will keep the marriage strong. When this custom is observed, the bride is said to be born again.

In the Synagogue

On a new moon, after the normal Torah reading for that day, Numbers 28:1-15, Psalm 104, and the Hallel (Psalms 113-118) would be read.

> And in the beginnings of your months ye shall offer a burnt offering unto the LORD; two young bullocks, and one ram, seven lambs of the first year without spot; and three tenth deals of flour *for* a meat offering, mingled with oil, for one bullock; and two tenth deals of flour *for* a meat offering, mingled with oil, for one ram; and a several tenth deal of flour mingled with oil *for* a meat offering unto one lamb; *for* a burnt offering of a sweet savour, a sacrifice made by fire unto the LORD. And their drink offerings shall be half an hin of wine unto a bullock, and the third *part* of an hin unto a ram, and a fourth *part* of an hin unto a lamb: this *is* the burnt offering of every month throughout the months of the year. And one kid of the goats for a sin offering unto the LORD shall be offered, beside

the continual burnt offering, and his drink offering.
Numbers 28:11-15

Bless the LORD, O my soul. O LORD my God, Thou
art very great; Thou art clothed with honour and
majesty. Who coverest *Thyself* with light as *with* a
garment: who stretchest out the heavens like a
curtain: who layeth the beams of His chambers in the
waters: who maketh the clouds His chariot: who
walketh upon the wings of the wind: who maketh His
angels spirits; His ministers a flaming fire: *who* laid
the foundations of the earth, *that* it should not be
removed for ever. Thou coveredst it with the deep as
with a garment: the waters stood above the mountains.
At Thy rebuke they fled; at the voice of Thy thunder
they hasted away. They go up by the mountains; they
go down by the valleys unto the place which Thou
hast founded for them. Thou hast set a bound that
they may not pass over; that they turn not again to
cover the earth. He sendeth the springs into the
valleys, *which* run among the hills. They give drink to
every beast of the field: the wild asses quench their
thirst. By them shall the fowls of the heaven have
their habitation, *which* sing among the branches. He
watereth the hills from His chambers: the earth is
satisfied with the fruit of Thy works. He causeth the
grass to grow for the cattle, and herb for the service of
man: that he may bring forth food out of the earth;
and wine *that* maketh glad the heart of man, *and* oil to
make *his* face to shine, and bread *which* strengtheneth
man's heart. The trees of the LORD are full *of sap;*
the cedars of Lebanon, which He hath planted; where
the birds make their nests: *as for* the stork, the fir
trees *are* her house. The high hills *are* a refuge for the
wild goats; *and* the rocks for the conies. He appointed
the moon for seasons: the sun knoweth his going

down. Thou makest darkness, and it is night: wherein all the beasts of the forest do creep *forth*. The young lions roar after their prey, and seek their meat from God. The sun ariseth, they gather themselves together, and lay them down in their dens. Man goeth forth unto his work and to his labour until the evening. O LORD, how manifold are Thy works! in wisdom hast Thou made them all: the earth is full of Thy riches. *So is* this great and wide sea, wherein *are* things creeping innumerable, both small and great beasts. There go the ships: *there is* that leviathan, *whom* Thou hast made to play therein. These wait all upon Thee; that Thou mayest give *them* their meat in due season. *That* Thou givest them they gather: Thou openest Thine hand, they are filled with good. Thou hidest Thy face, they are troubled: Thou takest away their breath, they die, and return to their dust. Thou sendest forth Thy spirit, they are created: and Thou renewest the face of the earth. The glory of the LORD shall endure for ever: the LORD shall rejoice in His works. He looketh on the earth, and it trembleth: He toucheth the hills, and they smoke. I will sing unto the LORD as long as I live: I will sing praise to my God while I have my being. My meditation of Him shall be sweet: I will be glad in the LORD. Let the sinners be consumed out of the earth, and let the wicked be no more. Bless thou the LORD, O my soul. Praise ye the LORD. *Psalms 104:1-35*

Ninth of Av,
Tisha B'Av

תשע באב

Tammuz						
S	M	T	W	T	F	S
		1	2	3	4	5
6	7	8	9	10	11	12
13	14	15	16	17	18	19
20	21	22	23	24	25	26
27	28	29				

Av						
S	M	T	W	T	F	S
			1	2	3	4
5	6	7	8	9	10	11
12	13	14	15	16	17	18
19	20	21	22	23	24	25
26	27	28	29	30		

The ninth day of the month of Av is not connected with rituals preformed on any of the ancient messianic festivals, but one can see a pattern when looking at history. Tisha B'Av, as it is called, is the date when the first and second temples were destroyed. Legend suggests it was also the date when Antiochus Epiphanes sacrificed a pig in the Jerusalem Temple, desecrating it. Many other tragic events have occured to the Jewish people on the ninth of Av. The following quotes are from the Codex Judaica by Rabbi Mattis Kantor.

Yaakov's [Jacob] subsequent confrontation with Eisav [Esau] (on his return to Canaan) was on the 9th of Av. *Codex Judaica p. 62*

Mose [Moses] sent the spies on the 29th of Sivan, and they returned, with bad news, on the 8th of Av. That night (9th of Av), Bnei Yisrael [children of Israel] bemoaned their plight, and were condemned to spend forty years in the desert. *Codex Judaica p. 78*

Yirmihahu [Jeremiah] had cursed the day he was born (which was the 9th of Av), because he despised being the prophet of doom for the land and the people that he loved. *Codex Judaica p. 103*

The attack on Yerushalayim [Jerusalem] was led by Nebuzradan, one of Nebuchadnetzar's ministers, and on the 9th of Tammuz the walls of Yerushalayim were penetrated. On the 17th of Tammuz the sacrifices ceased in the Beit Hamikdash [Jerusalem temple]... On Friday, the 7th of Av the enemy entered the Beit Hamikdash [Jerusalem temple], where they feasted and vandalized until late in the 9th [607 BC], when they set the structure afire. The fires burned for 24 hours. *Codex Judaica p. 103*

On the 17th of Tammuz the walls in Yerushalayim [Jerusalem] were penetrated, and the Romans advanced with difficulty, until they reached the Beit Hamikdash [Jerusalem temple] and set fire in it, on the 9th of Av, 3829 [AD 70]. *Codex Judaica p. 135*

Roman Governor, Tirentius Rufus I, ...plowed-under the whole city of Yerushalayim, and the site of the Beit Hamikdash, on the 9th of Av [AD 71].
Codex Judaica p. 142

'Bar Kockba' died in the battle, together with vast numbers of Jews (580,000). Many more died of starvation and many more were killed when Betar fell, on the 9th of Av (Tisha B'Av) [AD 130].
Codex Judaica p. 145

On Tisha B'av (9th of Av) in [AD] 1290, England became the first European country to completely expel all Jews from its borders. Sixteen thousand Jews left, most settled in Germany and some provinces of France. *Codex Judaica p. 190*

The Jews of France were arrested, their property was confiscated, and they were expelled in [AD] 1306, on the day after Tisha B'av [9th of Av].
Codex Judaica p. 200

Hundreds of Jews were massacred in Catalonia (a province of Spain) on the day after Tisha B'Av [AD 1358]. *Codex Judaica p. 204*

Most of the Jews -- who has left Spain by the 9th of Av [AD 1492] -- settled in Turkey, North Africa, and Italy. *Codex Judaica p. 211*

Three thousand Jews were killed in Staro-Konstantinov (Poland) on Tisha B'Av (9th of Av) [AD 1648].
Codex Judaica p. 230

All Jews were expelled from Austria... and the last Jews left Vienna on Tisha B'Av [9th of Av, AD 1670]. *Codex Judaica p. 240*

Germany declared war on Russia on Tisha B'Av [9th of Av, AD 1914] which marked the opening of the Eastern European front of World War I. *Codex Judaica p. 275*

The mass deportation of Jews from the Warsaw ghetto to the DEATH CAMPS began on Erev Tisha B'Av [9th of Av, AD 1942], at a daily rate of 5,000 or more... more than 200 Jews were killed in Ivye (Poland-Lithuania) on the 9th of Av (Tisha B'Av). *Codex Judaica p. 290*

17th of Tammuz

Associated with the ninth of Av is another date: the seventeenth of Tammuz.

When they [Syrians under Antiochus Epiphanes] gained a more strategic foothold in Yerushalayim [Jerusalem] itself, they completely stopped the holy services. Apustomus, one of the Syrian leaders, burned the Sefer Torah on the 17th of Tammuz. *Codex Judaica p. 124*

On the 17th of Tammuz the sacrifices ceased in the Beit Hamikdash [Jerusalem temple]. *Codex Judaica p. 103*

Events that occurred on the 9th of Av

1453 BC	The 40 years' wandering began
607 BC	Babylonians destroyed Solomon's Temple
166 BC	Antiochus Epiphanies defiled the second temple
AD 70	Romans destroyed the second temple
AD 71	Romans plowed under Jerusalem
AD 130	Bar Kockba was defeated and Israel dispersed
AD 1290	England expelled Jews
AD 1306	France expelled Jews
AD 1358	Catalonia (Spanish) massacre occurred
AD 1492	Spain expelled Jews
AD 1648	Poland massacre occurred
AD 1670	Austria expelled Jews
AD 1914	WWI Began
AD 1942	Nazi deportation to death camps began

Purim

פורים

Adar						
S	M	T	W	T	F	S
			1	2	3	4
5	6	7	8	9	10	11
12	13	14	15	16	17	18
19	20	21	22	23	24	25
26	27	28	29	30		

Nissan						
S	M	T	W	T	F	S
					1	2
3	4	5	6	7	8	9
10	11	12	13	14	15	16
17	18	19	20	21	22	23
24	25	26	27	28	29	30

The Festival of Purim commemorates the events that took place in the book of Esther. The book of Esther records the story of a decree made by the Persian king to have all the Jews slaughtered, and how God, though Esther, stopped this from occurring.

The interesting thing about these events is the typology referring to the Messiah. In Esther 3:13 the date decreed for the massacre was Adar 13. Even though this massacre was attempted, God gave the Jews victory over the

Persians. Esther 9:21-22 states the Festival of Purim was created on the 14th and 15th of Adar to commemorate the victory of the Jews over their enemies.

But if we look closely at the story, we see that Haman, a type of Antichrist, wanted to kill the Jews and tricked the king into making the decree.

Esther 3:7 recorded that the actual date the decree was created was the 13th of Nisan. In Esther 3:12, upon hearing about the decree, Esther asked all the Jews to fast with her for three days. This brings us to the 16th of Nisan, when Esther makes a banquet for the king and Haman. She then asked them to come back the next day for another banquet. This would be the 17th of Nisan, when she revealed what took place. On the 17th of Nisan Haman was killed and the King made another decree to save the Jews. The King gave his signet ring to Mordecai (a type of Jesus) who took Haman's place ruling the kingdom.

Haman and Pharaoh, who both typify Satan, were destroyed on the Nisan 17. Because of the Resurrection, which occurred on Nisan 17, Satan and the power of sin is destroyed over us.

Red Heifer

הפרה אדמה

The ritual most commonly referred to as the "ashes of the red heifer" is recorded in the book of Numbers.

And the LORD spake unto Moses and unto Aaron, saying, This *is* the ordinance of the law which the LORD hath commanded, saying, Speak unto the children of Israel, that they bring thee a red heifer without spot, wherein *is* no blemish, *and* upon which never came yoke: and ye shall give her unto Eleazar the priest, that he may bring her forth without the camp, and *one* shall slay her before his face: and Eleazar the priest shall take of her blood with his finger, and sprinkle of her blood directly before the tabernacle of the congregation seven times: and *one* shall burn the heifer in his sight; her skin, and her flesh, and her blood, with her dung, shall he burn: and the priest shall take cedar wood, and hyssop, and scarlet, and cast *it* into the midst of the burning of the heifer. Then the priest shall wash his clothes, and he shall bathe his flesh in water, and afterward he shall come into the camp, and the priest shall be unclean until the even. And he that burneth her shall wash his clothes in water, and bathe his flesh in water, and shall be unclean until the even. And a man *that is* clean shall gather up the ashes of the heifer, and lay *them* up without the camp in a clean place, and it shall be kept for the congregation of the children of Israel for a water of separation: it *is* a purification for sin.
Numbers 19:1-9

The details of this ritual are given in the Mishna, Parah Adamah 3.

Requirements

The red heifer must be without blemish, which means it can't have one hair that is white or black. She can't have even one root of a hair that is not red. She must be a red Angus that is red from one end to the other, even the skin on the nose and around the eyes. She can't have even one blemish, wart, mole, scratch, or scar of any kind. She can never have had a broken bone. No yoke manes, plough, rope, or blanket, and no one can have ridden her, etc. She must be three years old by the Jewish chronology (which starts at conception), two years old by our standards. At two years old the heifer would weight about 1,200 pounds. When she is slaughtered she must be outside the camp but be looking directly into the holy place (able to see the veil in the temple) so she must be directly east of the temple.

She can't touch anything unclean like a bone or a grave, so a special bridge has to be built for her to cross from the temple though the Eastern Gate over the Kidron valley (valley of death) where the dead are buried, to the Mount of Olives, called the mountain of the Messiah, where a special mikva, (baptismal) and altar had been built just for her.

The wood for the sacrifice is made up of cedar, pine, cypress, and pieces of smooth fig wood. There have been nine red heifer sacrifices in the last 3,500 years. The next one will be the tenth red heifer sacrifice. The Talmud states that the tenth and last heifer will be prepared by the Messiah. Whether this is true or not, it shows a belief that only ten red heifer sacrifices will occur for all time. So the tenth shows the coming of Messiah is drawing near.

Miracles of the Red Heifer
When the sacrifices begin, several miraculous things will occur that show God is pleased with the sacrifice.

1. One priest will gently pick her up and lay her on the altar.
2. When she is burned there will be no smell, no flies, no buzzards or vultures will come around.
3. The smoke will be white and go straight up no matter which direction the breeze is blowing or how much of a breeze there will be.

The priest will slit the throat of the heifer and catch the blood in a special container called a mizdrok. He will then sprinkle the blood seven times toward the temple.

The carcass will be set afire; and when it bursts open, the priest will take hyssop, cedar wood (a red wood), and scarlet wool and place them inside the opening of the heifer. When it is completely burnt to ashes, another priest will collect the ashes with a special shovel created only for that purpose and place the ashes in a special clay container.

These ashes, when added to the *myim hyim*, or living water, create a water of purification. We see this in John 2, when Jesus used some of these purification jars to turn the water into wine for the wedding.

The Return of the Messiah
The red heifer sacrifice might give us a picture of the Messiah standing on the Mount of Olives when He returns. The mountain will split in two, possibly creating a bridge so He may cross over to the temple clean (without touching the dead).

And his feet shall stand in that day upon the mount of Olives, which *is* before Jerusalem on the east, and the mount of Olives shall cleave in the midst thereof toward the east and toward the west, *and there shall be* a very great valley; and half of the mountain shall remove toward the north, and half of it toward the south. *Zechariah 14:4*

Wedding Ceremony

Like all the major ceremonies in the Jewish culture, the wedding ceremony conveys prophecy to us as well.

Betrothal - Shitre Erusin

A Jewish wedding has two stages to it. The first is called a betrothal or espousal. A contract or covenant, called the *Shitre Erusin*, is drawn up and the bride price is paid. The groom then returns to his father's house and builds a home for himself and his bride. When the father is satisfied that all things are finished, he instructs his son to go get his bride and bring her to the chuppah, or wedding canopy, for the actual wedding ceremony.

Kiddushin - Ketubah

The second stage of the wedding is called *Kiddushin*, where the actual marriage ceremony takes place.

In a Jewish wedding there are two witnesses, one assigned to the bride and the other assigned to the bridegroom. These help the bride and groom prepare for the fulfillment of the ceremony. The witnesses are also called the "friends of the bridegroom." This is most likely the source of the modern custom of having a best man and a maid of honor. The witness assigned to the bride escorts her to the chuppah where the ceremony takes place.

Before the bride and groom step under the chuppah, the bride circles the groom three times. This practice is taken from Hosea and referenced in Jeremiah.

> And I will betroth thee unto Me for ever; yea, I will betroth thee unto Me in righteousness, and in

judgment, and in lovingkindness, and in mercies. I will even betroth thee unto Me in faithfulness: and thou shalt know the LORD. *Hosea 2:19-20*

How long wilt thou go about, O thou backsliding daughter? For the LORD hath created a new thing in the earth, a woman shall compass a man... Behold, the days come, saith the LORD, that I will make a new covenant with the house of Israel, and with the house of Judah: not according to the covenant that I made with their fathers in the day *that* I took them by the hand to bring them out of the land of Egypt; which My covenant they brake, although I was an husband unto them, saith the LORD: but this *shall be* the covenant that I will make with the house of Israel; after those days, saith the LORD, I will put My law in their inward parts, and write it in their hearts; and will be their God, and they shall be My people.
Jeremiah 31:22, 31-33

Now with the first (old) covenant, the Shitre Erusin, fulfilled, it is set aside and a New Covenant, called the *Ketubah*, is drawn up allowing the groom to take his bride home.

According to ancient custom, the bride and groom would leave the wedding party, enter a private room, and consummate their marriage. The groom would then tell the friend of the bridegroom, who was waiting and listening at the door, that a marriage was made in Israel. The friend of the bridegroom would then announce to all the guests that the marriage was complete. And all would rejoice. The honeymoon would last for seven days. (See Genesis 29:27)

Ancient Messianic Festivals

The ancient rabbis taught this was a picture of God betrothing Israel by giving her the Ten Commandments at Mount Sinai.

In Exodus 19:19 Moses escorted the children of Israel to Mt. Sinai to enter into a relationship with God. Jeremiah refers to this event as an espousal.

> Go and cry in the ears of Jerusalem, saying, Thus saith the LORD; I remember thee, the kindness of thy youth, the love of thine espousals, when thou wentest after Me in the wilderness, in a land *that was* not sown. *Jeremiah 2:2*

New Testament - New Covenant
We can see by the language of Jesus, John the Baptist, and the apostle Paul that the Old Covenant was replaced by the New Covenant. And we are now waiting for Jesus to return and take His bride, the church, to the wedding chuppah for a seven-year honeymoon.

John the Baptist stated he was the friend of the bridegroom that waited to hear and rejoice.

> Ye yourselves bear me witness, that I said, I am not the Christ, but that I am sent before Him. He that hath the bride is the bridegroom: but the friend of the bridegroom, which standeth and heareth Him, rejoiceth greatly because of the bridegroom's voice: this my joy therefore is fulfilled. *John 3:28-29*

This tells us that the Rapture of the church is the catching away of the Messiah's bride, and the wedding supper of the Lamb occurs at that point. We will be gone for seven years, then return to earth with the Messiah.

In My Father's house are many mansions: if *it were* not *so,* I would have told you. I go to prepare a place for you. And if I go and prepare a place for you, I will come again, and receive you unto Myself; that where I am, *there* ye may be also. And whither I go ye know, and the way ye know. *John 14:2-4*

John answered and said, A man can receive nothing, except it be given him from heaven. Ye yourselves bear me witness, that I said, I am

Two Witnesses

Moses and Elijah
Joshua and Zerubbabel
Simeon and Anna
Revelation's two witnesses

not the Christ, but that I am sent before him. He that hath the bride is the bridegroom: but the friend of the bridegroom, which standeth and heareth Him, rejoiceth greatly because of the bridegroom's voice: this my joy therefore is fulfilled. *John 3:27-29*

In Jesus' parable of the wedding supper, the angels gather the elect from the four corners. The bride consists of those who are resurrected and raptured. The guests are those who make it through the Tribulation. Those without a wedding garment are those who tried to please God without accepting the Messiah and those with proper attire are those who accepted the Messiah. This corresponds with the Sheep and Goat Judgment in Matthew 25.

Tribulation Period Outline

The First 3.5 Years

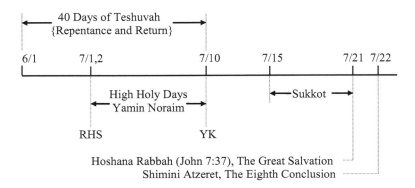

The fall festivals begin with the forty days of Teshuvah beginning on Elul 1, which teaches about the time of the return of the Messiah. Rosh Hashanah (RHS) is on the first and second of Tishrei, and teaches about the Resurrection and the Rapture. The Day of Atonement, called Yom Kippur (YK) is on the tenth of Tishrei and teaches about the Second Coming. The Days of Awe (Yamin Noraim) are the seven days between Rosh Hashanah and Yom Kippur which teaches about the tribulation period. Sukkot teaches about the millennial reign and Hoshana Rabbah teaches about the end of the millennial reign. Shimini Atzeret teaches about eternity and the New Jerusalem.

From the prophecy of the seventy weeks, found in Daniel 9, we are told there would be sixty-nine weeks of years (483 years) from the decree to rebuild the temple to the death of the Messiah. The decree was given on March 14, 444 BC. The Messiah died on April 6, AD 32. Only if we used the sacred Jewish calendar of 360 days per year, do the calculations come out correctly. This is the same method that accurately predicted the return of the Jews to Israel on May 14, AD 1948 and their taking of the Temple Mount on June 7, AD 1967. See *Ancient Prophecies Revealed* for details.

This means that the tribulation period is 2520 days split into two sections of 1260 days each. If it ends on a Day of Atonement, the middle date would fall on Nisan 10 and the beginning would fall on another Day of Atonement. This means the Rapture / Resurrection, which falls on a Rosh Hashanah, would occur about a week before the Antichrist enforces the seven-year peace covenant.

What could this week be for? There are 364 weeks in a seven-year period, which is about the same ratio as a half-an-hour for a real week. Destruction is held back for one week until the 144,000 are sealed. The silence in heaven for about a half an hour might typify a week in real time. See Revelation 7:1-8 and 8:1.

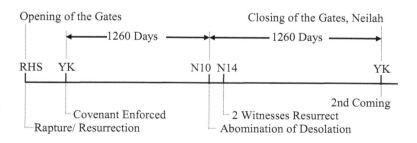

The last days begin with the Rapture on Rosh Hashanah (RHS), the opening of the gates.

Once the Days of Awe (Yamin Noraim) begin, the covenant is ratified and enforced. The Jews take full control of the Temple Mount and offer sacrifices on the Temple Mount to cleanse it, just like they did in Ezra 3:6. Then they begin construction of the temple itself. The two witnesses are revealed and begin their three-and-a-half-year time of witnessing, clothed in sackcloth. The 144,000 Jews become believers in reaction to seeing the Rapture/Resurrection. They are then sealed and begin their ministry as in Ezekiel 9.

The two witnesses prophecy for this same 1260-day-period, clothed in sackcloth, warning the people that Jesus is the Messiah and not to listen to the Antichrist. Israel rebuilds her temple under the leadership of the two witnesses and begins the temple sacrifices. The Antichrist must kill them to be able to enter the temple and place his image in the holy place.

The Antichrist kills the two witnesses when he begins his persecution of believers. This is when believing Israelis flee to the wilderness for 1260 days.

And the woman fled into the wilderness, where she hath a place prepared of God, that they should feed her there a thousand two hundred *and* threescore days. *Revelation 12:6*

The two witnesses are killed on Nisan 10 and lie in the street for three and a half days, then resurrect (Revelation 11:11). This places their resurrection on Nisan 14. This is the date of the Messiah's death and the resurrection of believers in Matthew.

Jesus, when He had cried again with a loud voice, yielded up the ghost. And, behold, the veil of the temple was rent in twain from the top to the bottom; and the earth did quake, and the rocks rent; and the graves were opened; and many bodies of the saints which slept arose, *Matthew 27:50-52*

The Second 3.5 Years

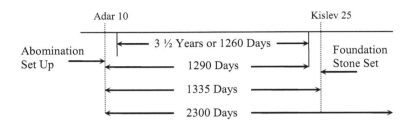

Daniel and Revelation teach that from the time the persecution begins to the Second Coming will be 1260 days, or a time, time, and a half a time. There will be 1290 days from the time the abomination is set up to the Second Coming and 1335 days from the abomination to laying the foundation stone of the new millennial temple. The millennial temple will be dedicated and operational 2300 days after the abomination is set up.

> And from the time *that* the daily *sacrifice* shall be taken away, and the abomination that maketh desolate set up, *there shall be* a thousand two hundred and ninety days. Blessed *is* he that waiteth, and cometh to the thousand three hundred and five and thirty days. *Daniel 12:11-12*

> ...by him the daily *sacrifice* was taken away, ...Unto two thousand and three hundred days; then shall the sanctuary be cleansed. *Daniel 8:11,14*

The Antichrist will kill the two witnesses and set up his idol in the temple on Adar 10. Thirty days later, on Nisan 10, the exact middle of the tribulation, he will begin a massive persecution of Jewish believers. Followers of the teachings of Jesus the Messiah will heed His instruction from Matthew 24:16 and flee to the mountains. Daniel 11:41 says Jordan (anciently called Edom, Moab, and Ammon) will escape out of the Antichrist's hands. In Jordan, safe from the Antichrist's hands, is the ancient city of Petra. Many believe the Jews will flee to this city.

There is a Dead Sea Scroll called the Zadokite fragment, often referred to as the Damascus document. Among other things, it mentions that after the city of Damascus is destroyed (as prophesied in Isaiah 17), an underground cavern will be opened up and the ancient tabernacle will be found and taken back to Jerusalem by the descendants of the priest Zadok. Many believe that when the Antichrist defiles the Jerusalem temple with his abominable idol, the true Jewish believers will flee to Petra with the tabernacle and continue the temple rituals in their purity.

Passages like Isaiah 16 and 42 speak of a place of refuge called Selah. Selah is an ancient Hebrew word for the city of Petra.

So 1290 days after the abomination is set up, the Messiah will return to earth on a Yom Kippur. Forty-five days later (the 1335 days) the foundation stone for the new temple will be laid on Kislev 25, the first day of Hanukkah. Then two years, ten months, and twenty days after the Second Coming (the 2300 days), the Temple will be dedicated by the Messiah Himself!

Appendices

Appendix A
Halloween

Cheshvan						
S	M	T	W	T	F	S
1	2	3	4	5	6	7
8	9	10	11	12	13	14
15	16	17	18	19	20	21
22	23	24	25	26	27	28
29						

We read in Genesis that the world-wide flood that destroyed all of mankind except Noah and his family occurred on Cheshvan 17.

In the six hundredth year of Noah's life, in the second month, the seventeenth day of the month, the same day were all the fountains of the great deep broken up, and the windows of heaven were opened.
Genesis 7:11

This was adopted by many post-flood nations as a New Year's Day and a kind of Memorial Day. Most ancient cultures went by a lunar calendar, like the Jews, and commemorated it on the full moon, or middle of their month. The Celts, druids and Wiccans, still have their New Year's rites on this full moon. Halloween is celebrated at the end of October to fit the American solar calendar.

As the gentile nations grew more and more pagan (see *Ancient Paganism* for details), Halloween became a satanic holiday. The *Ancient Book of Jasher* records that when Sodom and Gomorrah grew more occultic they started celebrating the four pagan holidays of which Halloween was the chief.

> In those days all the people of Sodom and Gomorrah, and of the whole five cities, were exceedingly wicked and sinful against the Lord and they provoked the Lord with their abominations, and they strengthened in aging abominably and scornfully before the Lord, and their wickedness and crimes were in those days great before the Lord. And they had in their land a very extensive valley, about half a day's walk, and in it there were fountains of water and a great deal of herbage surrounding the water. And all the people of Sodom and Gomorrah went there **four times in the year**, with their wives and children and all belonging to them, and they rejoiced there with timbrels and dances. *Ancient Book of Jasher 18:11-13*

The kings of Israel and Judah brought paganism into the Holy Land. When the ten northern tribes separated from the two southern tribes, Jeroboam, king of Israel, did not want all of his people to travel to the Jerusalem temple and pay tithes there. He created two new places to worship, one in Bethel and the other in Dan. He created calf-like gods to be worshiped there and reinstated Halloween (the full moon of the eighth month) as his new feast.

> Whereupon the king took counsel, and made two calves *of* gold, and said unto them, It is too much for you to go up to Jerusalem: behold thy gods, O Israel, which brought thee up out of the land of Egypt. And he set the one in Bethel, and the other put he in Dan. And this thing became a sin: for the people went *to*

worship before the one, *even* unto Dan. And he made an house of high places, and made priests of the lowest of the people, which were not of the sons of Levi. And Jeroboam ordained a feast in the eighth month, on the fifteenth day of the month, like unto the feast that *is* in Judah, and he offered upon the altar. So did he in Bethel, sacrificing unto the calves that he had made: and he placed in Bethel the priests of the high places which he had made. So he offered upon the altar which he had made in Bethel the **fifteenth day of the eighth month**, *even* in the month which he had devised of his own heart; and ordained a feast unto the children of Israel: and he offered upon the altar, and burnt incense. *1 Kings 12:28-33*

Since Hanukkah was created by man and yet used by God for typological prophecy like His seven festivals, and God is the one who caused the Flood to occur on the date it did, we need to consider that it may have a part in the chronology of end time events.

Appendix B
Types and Shadows Charts

The concept of types and shadows is taught throughout the New Testament. In this first chart are the types and shadows revealed by the apostle Paul in the Book of Hebrews.

Types Defined in Hebrews

Vs		
Heb 4:9	Weekly Sabbath	Age of Grace (resting from Mosaic works)
Heb 9:2	Outer tabernacle / Holy place	The Church
Heb 9:2	Lamp stand	
Heb 9:2	Table of Showbread	
Heb 9:3	Holy of Holies	Throne room of God / Heaven
Heb 9:3	Second veil (split in two)	All go boldly before the throne of God (Exodus 26:31-33) Mat 27:51
Heb 9:4	Altar of incense	Prayers of the saints Rev 8:4
Heb 9:4	Ark of the Covenant	
Heb 9:4	Golden jar of manna	Bread of life, hidden manna Rev 2:17 (1 Kings 8:9)
Heb 9:4	Aaron's rod	(Num. 17:1-8)
Heb 9:4	Tablets of the Covenant	(Deut. 10:1-5)
Heb 9:5	Cherubim	Four living creatures
Heb 9:5	Mercy seat – covering	
Heb 9:7	Yom Kippur ritual	The Messiah and the Antichrist
Heb 9:13	Ashes of the red heifer	Christ's atoning sacrifice
Heb 9:19	Scarlet wool & hyssop	Made clean by the blood of the Lamb
Heb 10:22	Water basin	Pure conscience (1Pet 3:21
Heb 13:2	Red heifer burned outside the camp	Jesus crucified outside Jerusalem

The Apostle Paul and our Lord Jesus gave several examples of prophecy based on types and shadows. We can see how these fit nicely with our study of the messianic festivals. This first chart shows things mentioned as types. The second chart shows things from the Old Testament that might be a type or shadow.

Ancient Messianic Festivals

Other Types Defined in the NT

Eph 2:13	Middle wall of partition broken down	Jew & Gentile equally enter the throne room
2Cor 3:7	Moses' glory faded from his face	The old covenant/Law would fade
2Cor 3:14	Veil over Moses' face	Refuse to leave the Mosaic Covenant for Christ's
1Cor 10:3	Rock from which water flowed,	Represented Christ - Exodus 17:6
1Cor 10:3	Manna, cloud & sea-baptism	Salvation (1Pet 5:21
Jn 3:14	Brazen serpent (Num 21:8)	Jesus lifted up on the cross
Mt 12:40	Sign of Jonah	Jesus buried for three days
Gal 4:21	Sarah/Hagar	Old and new covenants- through man or God
Gal 4:21-31	Sinai symbolizes bondage	Legalism
Gal 4:21-31	New Jerusalem gives freedom	
Gal 4:21-31	Isaac	Child of promise - Gen 22:8,18
Gal 4:21-31	Ishmael	Child of bondage
Col 2:17	Food, drink, new moon, Sabbath, seven festivals	
Rom 5	Adam	Christ

Other Possible Types

Num 2	Israeli camp forms a cross	
Ex 17:9-12	Moses has to form a cross for Israelis to win a battle	
Num 20:8	Moses strikes rock instead of speaking to it	By his power not reliance on HS – Gal 3:1-3
	Moses breaking the Ten Commandments	New covenant coming Jesus replaces old with new
Num 35:28	Manslaughterers forgiven when current high priest dies	
Lev 10:1-2	Nadab & Abihu – strange fire	
2King 6:5	Axe floating - Elijah	
Ex 15:23	Wood to fix bitter water	The cross purifies
Daniel 2	Nebuchadnezzar's Image & 666	

Other Books by
Ken Johnson, Th.D.

Ancient Post-Flood History
Historical Documents That Point to a Biblical Creation.

This book is a Christian timeline of ancient post-Flood history based on Bible chronology, the early church fathers, and ancient Jewish and secular history. This can be used as a companion guide in the study of Creation Science.

Some questions answered: Who were the Pharaohs in the times of Joseph and Moses? When did the famine of Joseph occur? What Egyptian documents mention these? When did the Exodus take place? When did the Kings of Egypt start being called "Pharaoh" and why?

Who was the first king of a united Italy? Who was Zeus and where is he buried? Where did Shem and Ham rule and where are they buried?

How large was Nimrod's invasion force that set up the Babylonian Empire, and when did this invasion occur? What is Nimrod's name in Persian documents?

How can we use this information to witness to unbelievers?

Ancient Seder Olam
A Christian Translation of the 2000-year-old Scroll

This 2000-year-old scroll reveals the chronology from Creation through Cyrus' decree that freed the Jews in 536 BC. The *Ancient Seder Olam* uses biblical prophecy to prove its calculations of the timeline. We have used this technique to continue the timeline all the way to the reestablishment of the nation of Israel in AD 1948.

Using the Bible and rabbinical tradition, this book shows that the ancient Jews awaited King Messiah to fulfill the prophecy spoken of in Daniel, Chapter 9. The Seder answers many questions about the chronology of the books of Kings and Chronicles. It talks about the coming of Elijah, King Messiah's reign, and the battle of Gog and Magog.

This scroll and the Jasher scroll are the two main sources used in Ken's first book, *Ancient Post-Flood History*.

Ancient Prophecies Revealed
500 Prophecies Listed In Order Of When They Were Fulfilled

This book details over 500 biblical prophecies in the order they were fulfilled; these include pre-flood times though the First Coming of Jesus and into the Middle Ages. The heart of this book is the 53 prophecies fulfilled between 1948 and 2008. The last eleven prophecies between 2008 and the Tribulation are also given. All these are documented and interpreted from the Ancient Church Fathers.

The Ancient Church Fathers, including disciples of the twelve apostles, were firmly premillennial, pretribulational, and very pro-Israel.

Ancient Book of Jasher
Referenced in Joshua 10:13; 2 Samuel 1:18; 2 Timothy 3:8

There are thirteen ancient history books mentioned and recommended by the Bible. The Ancient Book of Jasher is the only one of the thirteen that still exists. It is referenced in Joshua 10:13; 2 Samuel 1:18; and 2 Timothy 3:8. This volume contains the entire 91 chapters plus a detailed analysis of the supposed discrepancies, cross-referenced historical accounts, and detailed charts for ease of use. As with any history book, there are typographical errors in the text but with three consecutive timelines running though the histories, it is very easy to arrive at the exact dates of recorded events. It is not surprising that this ancient document confirms the Scripture and the chronology given in the Hebrew version of the Old Testament, once and for all settling the chronology differences between the Hebrew Old Testament and the Greek Septuagint.

Third Corinthians
Ancient Gnostics and the End of the World

This little known, 2000-year-old Greek manuscript was used in the first two centuries to combat Gnostic cults. Whether or not it is an authentic copy of the original epistle written by the apostle Paul, it gives an incredible look into the cults that will arise in the Last Days.

It contains a prophecy that the same heresies that pervaded the first century church would return before the Second Coming of the Messiah.

Ancient Paganism
The Sorcery of the Fallen Angels

Ancient Paganism explores the false religion of the ancient pre-Flood world and its spread into the gentile nations after Noah's Flood. Quotes from the ancient church fathers, rabbis, and the Talmud detail the activities and beliefs of both Canaanite and New Testament era sorcery. This book explores how, according to biblical prophecy, this same sorcery will return before the Second Coming of Jesus Christ to earth. These religious beliefs and practices will invade the end time church and become the basis for the religion of the Antichrist. Wicca, Druidism, Halloween, Yule, meditation, and occultic tools are discussed at length.

The Rapture
The Pretribulational Rapture of the Church Viewed From the Bible and the Ancient Church

This book presents the doctrine of the pretribulational Rapture of the church. Many prophecies are explored with Biblical passages and terms explained.

Evidence is presented that proves the first century church believed the End Times would begin with the return of Israel to her ancient homeland, followed by the Tribulation and the Second Coming. More than fifty prophecies have been fulfilled since Israel became a state.

Evidence is also given that several ancient rabbis and at least four ancient church fathers taught a pretribulational Rapture. This book also gives many answers to the arguments midtribulationists and posttribulationists use. It is our hope this book will be an indispensable guide for debating the doctrine of the Rapture.

Ancient Epistle of Barnabas
His Life and Teaching

The Epistle of Barnabas is often quoted by the ancient church fathers. Although not considered inspired Scripture, it was used to combat legalism in the first two centuries AD. Besides explaining why the

Laws of Moses are not binding on Christians, the Epistle explains how many of the Old Testament rituals teach typological prophecy. Subjects explored are: Yom Kippur, the Red Heifer ritual, animal sacrifices, circumcision, the Sabbath, Daniel's visions and the end-time ten-nation empire, and the temple.

The underlying theme is the Three-Fold Witness. Barnabas teaches that mature Christians must be able to lead people to the Lord, testify to others about Bible prophecy fulfilled in their lifetimes, and teach creation history and creation science to guard the faith against the false doctrine of evolution. This is one more ancient church document that proves the first century church was premillennial and constantly looking for the Rapture and other prophecies to be fulfilled.

The Ancient Church Fathers
What the Disciples of the Apostles Taught

This book reveals who the disciples of the twelve apostles were and what they taught, from their own writings. It documents the same doctrine was faithfully transmitted to their descendants in the first few centuries and where, when, and by whom, the doctrines began to change. The ancient church fathers make it very easy to know for sure what the complete teachings of Jesus and the twelve apostles were.

You will learn, from their own writings, that the first century disciples taught about the various doctrines that divide our church today. You will learn what was discussed at the seven general councils and why. You will learn who were the cults and cult leaders that began to change doctrine and spread their heresy and how that became to be the standard teaching in the medieval church. A partial list of doctrines discussed in this book are:

Abortion	False gospels	Mary's assumption
Animals sacrifices	False prophets	Meditation
Antichrist	Foreknowledge	The Nicolaitans
Arminianism	Free will	Paganism
Bible or tradition	Gnostic cults	Predestination
Calvinism	Homosexuality	premillennialism
Circumcision	Idolatry	Purgatory
Deity of Jesus Christ	Islam	Psychology
Demons	Israel's return	Reincarnation
Euthanasia	Jewish food laws	Replacement theology
Evolution	Mary's virginity	Roman Catholicism

The Sabbath	Sin / Salvation	Transubstantiation
Salvation	The soul	Yoga
Schism of Nepos	Spiritual gifts	Women in ministry

Ancient Book of Daniel

The ancient Hebrew prophet Daniel lived in the fifth century BC and accurately predicted the history of the nation of Israel from 536 BC to AD 1948. He also predicted the date of the death of the Messiah to occur in AD 32, the date of the rebirth of the nation of Israel to occur in AD 1948, and the Israeli capture of the Temple Mount to take place in AD 1967! Commentary from the ancient rabbis and the first century church reveals how the messianic rabbis and the disciples of the apostles interpreted his prophecies.

Daniel also indicated where the Antichrist would come from, where he would place his international headquarters, and identified the three rebel nations that will attack him during the first three-and-a-half years of the Tribulation.

Ancient Epistles of John and Jude

This book provides commentary for the epistles of John and Jude from the ancient church fathers. It gives the history of the struggles of the first century church. You will learn which cults John and Jude were writing about and be able to clearly identify each heresy. You will also learn what meditation and sorcery truly are. At the end of each chapter is a chart contrasting the teaching of the church and that of the Gnostics. Included are master charts of the *doctrine of Christ*, the *commandments of Christ*, and the *teaching of the apostles*.

Learn the major doctrines that all Christians must believe:

Jesus is the only Christ	The Rapture
Jesus is the only Savior	Creationism
Jesus is the only begotten Son of God	Eternal life only by Jesus
Jesus is sinless	The sin nature
Jesus physically resurrected	Prophecy proves inspiration
Jesus will physically return to earth	Idolatry is evil
God is not evil	

For more information visit us at:

Biblefacts.org

Bibliography

Ken Johnson, *Ancient Prophecies Revealed*, Createspace, 2008
Ken Johnson, *Ancient Paganism*, Createspace, 2009
Ken Johnson, *Ancient Book of Jasher*, Createspace, 2008
Herbert Danby, *The Mishnah*, Oxford University Press, 1933
Ken Johnson, *Ancient Church Fathers*, Createspace, 2010
Mattis Kantor, *Codex Judaica*, Zichron Press, 2005
Moshe Weissman, *The Midrash Says: The Book of Sh'mos*, Benei Yakov Publications, 1995
Ken Johnson, *Ancient Seder Olam*, Createspace, 2006
Ken Johnson, *Ancient Post-Flood History*, Createspace, 2010
Eerdmans Publishing, *Ante-Nicene Fathers*, Eerdmans Publishing, 1886
Roland De Vaux, *Ancient Israel, Its Life and Institutions*, McGraw-Hill, 1961

Made in the USA
Lexington, KY
27 February 2014